beginner's guide to
Limit Hold'em

Byron Jacobs

D&B PUBLISHING

www.dandbpoker.com

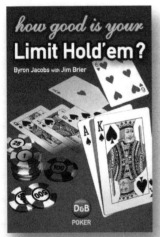

First published in 2006 by D & B Publishing, PO Box 18, Hassocks, West Sussex BN6 9WR

Copyright © 2006 Byron Jacobs

The right of Byron Jacobs to be identified as the author of this work has been asserted in accordance with the Copyrights, Designs and Patents Act 1988.

British Library Cataloguing-in-Publication Data
A catalogue record for this book is available from the British Library.

ISBN 1-904468-21-7

All sales enquiries should be directed to:
D & B Publishing, PO Box 18, Hassocks,
West Sussex BN6 9WR, UK

Tel: +44 (0)1273 834680, Fax: +44 (0)1273 831629,
e-mail: info@dandbpublishing.com,
Website: www.dandbpoker.com

Cover design by Horatio Monteverde.
Production by Navigator Guides.
Printed and bound in the US by Versa Press.

Contents

Chapter One

Why Play Poker?

- ♣ The Online Poker Revolution
- ♣ Hold'em Poker
- ♣ Show me the Money
- ♣ Developing a Feel
- ♣ The Scope of this Book

The Online Poker Revolution

Poker has witnessed an explosion of interest in recent years. The arrival of online cardrooms on the internet means that there are now thousands of cash games and tournaments available 24 hours a day at hundreds of different sites. The incredible interest that these sites generate can be seen from the valuation of nearly $5 billion which was attached to the leading online site, PartyPoker.com, when it floated in mid-2005.

The internet has made poker far, far more accessible than it ever was. The easy availability of online games means that anyone can play at any time. It is no longer necessary to seek out a cardroom in your local area, find your way over there and then possibly wait around until a free place becomes available. If you have a computer with an internet connection you can download software, register with a site and be playing poker within five minutes. And this is only to play your first game. Once you have installed the software and are registered then the next time you want to play you can be enjoying live action within 15 seconds.

Everyone is playing poker. I have played in online games with doctors, lawyers, social workers, midwives, housewives, students, celebrities, professional players, world champions and even one major Hollywood star. As with everything internet-related, online poker has integrated the world into a global village beyond anything that could have been anticipated by Marshall McLuhan.

A couple of years ago I was playing in a five-handed game. When you play online you use an alias (a handle) to identify yourself, but also give the area that you come from. Obviously players can lie about this but there seems no great incentive to do so. At the time I was residing in Hove in Sussex. My four opponents hailed from: Melbourne in Australia; San Francisco in the USA; Vancouver in Canada; and finally from Brunswick Square, which is approximately 150 yards from where I was living.

Serious Money

The 'World Championship' of the poker world is the World Series, which is held every summer in Las Vegas. In this event, players 'buy-in' with $10,000 and the accumulation of these entry fees makes up the prize pool. When a player loses their chips they are eliminated and play continues until one player has all the money. Prizes are typically paid out to the top 10% on a sliding scale with the winner receiving the lion's share.

In 2001, this event had 613 entries and the eventual winner, Juan Carlos Mortensen of Madrid, took home $1.5 million. The runner-up won just over $1 million. This was fairly typical of this tournament at the time. However, with the advent of online play it is now possible to enter qualifiers (known as *satellites*) and, by winning such an event, a player gets a prize of a 'free' buy-in to the World Series. These events have proved to be enormously popular and, in consequence, entries for the World Series have increased dramatically.

In 2003, there were 839 entries and the eventual winner was the wonderfully-named Chris Moneymaker of the US, who took home $2.5 million. The remarkable feature of his achievement was that this was the very first 'live' tournament he had played, and that he obtained his seat by winning a $40 qualifier on the internet!

By 2004 things had really taken off and at the start of play there were an astonishing 2,576 competitors – three times the number from the previous year. The winner was Greg Raymer of the US, who scooped $5 million for his victory. He too was an internet qualifier. Even the player finishing in fifth place took home over $1 million, and number 27 in the final lists won $120,000.

The 2005 event saw 5,661 entrants for the World Series with total prize money at nearly $53 million. This is, by far, the biggest ever prize fund for a sporting event. The winner, Joseph Hachem, walked away with $7.5 million, with the runner-up, Steve Dannenmann netting $4.5 million. Everyone who made it through to the last day's play and final table (nine players) pocketed a minimum of $1 million. Presumably it will not be long before the total prize money in this event tops $100 million.

Hold'em Poker

There are many different ways to play poker. Those of you who have not played for many years are probably familiar with the classic variants such as draw poker and seven-card stud. However, over the last two decades hold'em has become firmly established as the most popular form of poker. It is the most popular poker game played in casinos and it is also the most popular game played online. In this book I am going to give you a thorough grounding in the game of limit hold'em.

How does Hold'em Work?

Hold'em employs the concept of 'community cards' – cards which are shared by all players at the table. Every player is dealt two cards which comprise their hand, and then five cards are dealt face up in the centre of the table. These are the so-called community cards and are also known as *the board*. The aim of the game is to combine your two cards with the five board cards to make the best possible poker hand. To this end you are allowed to use either one or both of your hole cards. If, at the end of play, your hand is better than those of your opponents, then you get to win the pot. The other way to win a pot is to have all of your opponents fold (i.e. throw away their hands) before the showdown. Then you win regardless of your cards. It is permissible, but unlikely, that you would want to use neither of your hole cards. In that case you would be playing the board and nobody else could possibly have a weaker hand.

Why play Limit Hold'em?

As we already know, hold'em is the most popular form of

poker. If you want to get involved in the poker explosion then you will have to know how to play hold'em. The game played in all the major tournaments and, indeed, in the World Series is hold'em. Secondly, it is easier to learn than the other poker variants. The other most popular poker variant is Omaha and this game is, in a sense, a more complex version of hold'em.

What does 'Limit' mean?

'Limit' refers to the betting structure. There are three ways in which hold'em (and indeed all other poker games) can be played: no-limit, pot-limit and fixed limit (usually known simply as 'limit'). In no-limit, you are entitled to bet any amount of money at any time – the only caveat being that you must actually have that money on the table in front of you at the time. Suddenly delving into your wallet when you hit a big hand is, unsurprisingly, not allowed. Pot-limit allows you to bet any amount of money up to the current value of the pot. In limit your bet is a fixed unit which is defined by the level of the game.

This makes limit hold'em a simpler game (to learn at least) than pot- or no-limit. In these games, big bets can suddenly appear out of nowhere and the size of the pot can escalate alarmingly. This does not happen in limit. The pots can get big – and they frequently do – but this happens gradually and not as the result of one huge bet. Limit hold'em is a better game for beginners than the other variants. If you make a mistake in pot- and no-limit you are vulnerable to losing your entire stack on a single hand. If you make a mistake in limit play you will dribble away some money but a single hand will not wipe you out.

Betting Limits

Limit hold'em can be played at a wide variety of levels and online sites offer games ranging from those played for tiny amounts of money to those played for quite considerable sums. The level of the game is defined by two monetary amounts, the first being the *small bet* and the second being the *big bet*. The big bet is always precisely twice the size of the small bet. Thus typical games are $0.50-$1 limit hold'em, $2-$4 limit hold'em; $10-$20 limit hold'em; $40-$80 limit hold'em; and even $1,000-$2,000 limit hold'em. In his book, *The Professor, The Banker and the Suicide King*, Michael Craig catalogues private hold'em games that were played at limits of up to $100,000-$200,000.

As a beginning player I would, naturally, recommend that you start to play at a level where you are very comfortable with the potential losses. However, throughout this book I shall give examples of play from various different limits.

Show me the Money

Poker is all about money. Although social games are occasionally played for buttons, matchsticks, milk bottle tops or whatever, at the end of the day poker doesn't make much sense if you are not playing for money. All online sites offer *play money* games where you can try out the games playing purely for the fun of it. However, I would recommend that you only spend a small amount of time playing these games and only do this to familiarise yourself with the workings of the site and the game. The problem with playing when there is no money at stake is that there is no incentive (either for you or for your opponents) to try and play properly. It is crucial to develop a 'feel' for hold'em (there will be much more on this later) and this is impossible in such artificial situations.

I would strongly recommend that – once you are comfortable with your understanding of the game – you begin playing as soon as possible in cash games, even if they are for very small amounts. All sites spread a $0.50-$1 limit hold'em game and numerous sites offer *micro-limit* games, playing for sums such as $0.10-$0.20. A reasonable rule of thumb is that you need to sit down at a table with a stack which is approximately 25 times the big bet. Thus to sit in a $5-$10 game you need about $250. However, you can play at the $0.50-$1 limit with just

$25. If this is more than you want to risk, then a micro-limit game of $0.10-$0.20 would require a stack of just $5. Players who play cash games – regardless of how high or low the level – usually take them seriously. You need to be able to play your poker in a serious frame of mind against other serious players, and you won't get this experience from play money games.

Developing a Feel

My emphasis throughout this book will emphatically be to try and give you a *feel* for how to play the game of limit hold'em. When learning the game myself, I read a number of books and absorbed advice such as to only call from the button with a pair of fives if three or more players had already called before me. This I dutifully did – the only problem being – I had no idea why. I did not have a *feel* for what I was trying to achieve with this pair of fives, other than that it would be nice if another one popped up on the flop.

Here is another example. I would learn that when I was first to bet in the pot I should fold with A-10, but I should open with a raise when holding A-J, unless the game was very tight, in which case I should probably fold A-J too. However, if my A-J was suited, then I could play the hand. Really? How fascinating. What terrible calamity would befall me if I played this A-J offsuit in a tight game? Perhaps my computer would explode, or maybe someone would call the police. And, come to that, what is a tight game anyway? I certainly had no idea, and I firmly believe that such advice is more or less useless for beginning players.

A further reason to try and develop a feel is that online limit poker is played pretty fast. You usually have a maximum of 15-20 seconds to make your decisions. This may seem frighteningly fast right now, but once you get involved in the play you will see that many decisions are more or less automatic. You will find that 90% of plays at the table are made within a couple of seconds. If you use most of your time allowance for each decision you will soon irritate the other players at the table.

These players often have the attention span of a gnat, and cannot bear to go more than five seconds without getting their 'buzz' from the action. If you deprive them of this they will be quick to let you know in the chat box.

The Scope of this Book

This book will start with the absolute basics of poker. I am making just one assumption about readers – I will presume that you are familiar with a normal deck of 52 cards. I will assume no other poker knowledge on your part at all. Thus if you already have a little experience of limit hold'em, then you may view some of the earlier material as just brushing up on what you already know.

If you read this book thoroughly and take your time to absorb the information here, then you will emerge with a pretty reasonable understanding of limit hold'em. This will not make you a great player, but it will give you a good start and enable you to compete at the low levels without being at a disadvantage, even if everyone at your table is much more experienced than you.

Limit hold'em is very much a game where a thinking player will improve with experience. There are hundreds of thousands of people already playing poker either for a living or as a serious hobby. If you know either very little or nothing of poker but you would like to join them, then this book is a good place to start.

Chapter Two

The Ranking of the Hands

- ♣ Introduction
- ♣ Hand Rankings
- ♣ Exercise One
- ♣ Exercise Two

Introduction

Before we move on to explore the game of limit hold'em in detail, we need to ensure that you are completely familiar with the ranking of poker hands. The material in this chapter will do just that and also applies to any other poker variant that is played 'high', i.e. you are attempting to make the best possible hand. Such games include seven-card stud, draw poker and Omaha.

A poker hand is made up of five cards, and a higher-ranked hand beats a lower-ranked hand. There are various categories of poker hands and the ranking of these is as follows:

Possible Poker Hands
Royal Flush
Straight Flush
Four of a Kind
Full House
Flush
Straight
Three of a Kind
Two Pair
One Pair
High Card

Hand Rankings

We shall now examine each of the hand rankings in detail.

Royal Flush

A royal flush is the best possible hand. A flush means that all cards are of the same suit. A royal flush means that you hold precisely A-K-Q-J-10. The following are royal flushes:

All royal flushes are equal. A spade royal flush does not, for example beat a club royal flush.

Royal flushes are extremely rare. I have played around half a million online hold'em hands, and I think I have had two royal flushes.

Straight Flush

A straight flush consists of five cards of consecutive rank, all of the same suit. The ace can count 'high' or 'low', thus A♥-K♥-Q♥-J♥-10♥ is a straight flush (in fact – as we saw earlier – this is a royal flush), as is 5♣-4♣-3♣-2♣-A♣ (again all of the same suit).

The following hands are all straight flushes:

A higher ranking straight flush beats a lower ranking straight flush. Thus in the above three examples the best hand is the K♥-Q♥-J♥-10♥-9♥ and the weakest hand is the 5♣-4♣-3♣-2♣-A♣. In fact this latter hand is the lowest possible straight flush. However, if you do get it, don't be disappointed – it's still a pretty good hand!

As with royal flushes, two straight flushes of the same rank are equal. Unlike bridge, the suits are all equal. Note that having four cards that make up part of a straight flush plus a rogue card is no good. Thus the following hand

is almost a straight flush but is, in fact, almost completely worthless. In poker your straights and flushes need to be five-card hands. You get no prizes for near misses.

Four of a Kind

A four of a kind is a hand which consists of four cards of the same rank. The fifth card (or side card) can be any other card. Here are some examples:

Four of a kind is also known as quads. Thus the three hands given above are, respectively, quad kings, quad sixes and quad eights. Unsurprisingly, the kings are the best hand, followed by the eights and then the sixes. The side card is irrelevant, so the fact that the quad sixes are accompanied by the best side card – an ace – does not help their cause when they are competing against the kings and sixes. However...

The Kicker

The kicker is a fundamental concept in hold'em. If two players have the same basic hand – and this is not a five-card hand – then the best kicker (also known as the side card) counts. This can be decisive and can occur with four of a kind hands. Thus

beats

as the king ranks higher than the jack. You may be wondering how it is possible for two players to have so many sevens between them, bearing in mind that there are only four of them in the deck. The key point is that hold'em is a game that features community (shared) cards. Thus if the four sevens appear in the community cards then everyone has them and the kickers become crucial.

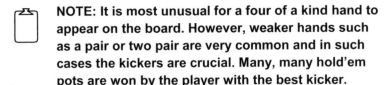 **NOTE: It is most unusual for a four of a kind hand to appear on the board. However, weaker hands such as a pair or two pair are very common and in such cases the kickers are crucial. Many, many hold'em pots are won by the player with the best kicker.**

Full House

The next best hand after four of a kind is a full house. A full house consists of three cards of the same rank accompanied by a pair of the same rank. The following are examples of full houses:

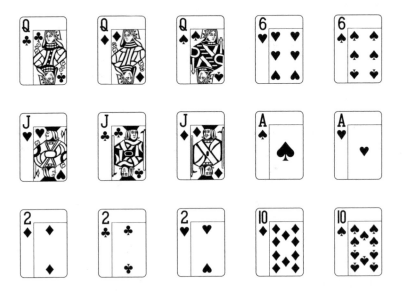

The ranking of a full house is determined by the rank of the *three of a kind*. Thus the above three hands are in order of merit with the queens full house beating the jacks full house and both of these hands beating the twos full house. Although the jacks have the best accompanying pair, this does not help them to overtake the queens.

A common way to completely describe a full house is to say 'queens full of sixes'. Obviously this refers to the first hand above. The others are jacks full of aces and twos full of tens.

If two players share the same *three of a kind* then the best pair acts as the tie-breaker. Thus

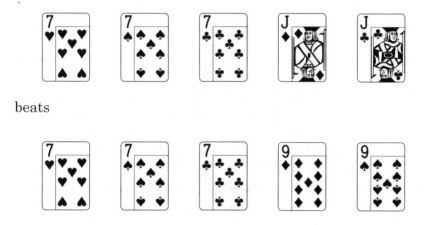

beats

as the jacks outrank the nines. Note that full houses are 'five-card' hands and so there is never any involvement of a kicker.

Flush

A flush is a hand which consists of all five cards being of the same suit. Four cards is not good enough. As we have already seen, you must have all five cards in the same suit – near misses counting for nothing. The following are flush hands:

The ranking of flush hands is determined by the highest card, followed by the second highest, third highest etc. Thus the strongest of the three above hands is the club flush which is led by an ace. The next best is the diamond flush. If we consider this hand against the spade flush we can see that they are both led by the Q-J combination. However, in this instance we have to consider the third card – and when we do, we see that the 10♦ outranks the 6♠.

It does not matter how many high cards you have in a suit – it is the highest card that counts. Thus although

might look a whole lot more impressive than

the latter hand takes it due to the simple fact that the ace beats the king.

Straight

Ranking immediately below the flush is the straight. Some readers might be familiar with the game of brag which is a sort of very basic form of poker played with just three cards. In brag a straight beats a flush, but in poker the flush always outranks the straight.

A straight consists of five cards in sequence and the ace can count high or low. The following hands are all straights.

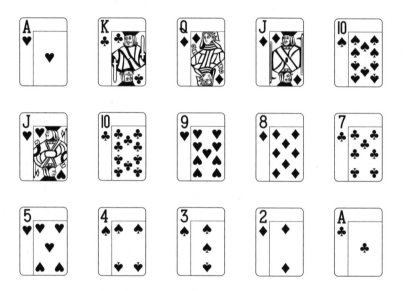

The top straight is sometimes known as the *broadway* straight and the lowest straight is sometimes referred to as the *wheel*. You will not be surprised to learn that, of the above three straights, the straight down from the ace beats the one down from the jack which in turn beats the wheel.

Three of a Kind

Three of a kind is a hand which features three cards of the same rank and where the other two do not share the same rank. It is thus a full house without the pair. Here are some examples:

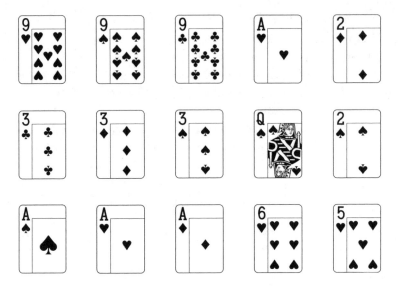

Unsurprisingly, the best hand here are the three aces, followed by the three nines and finally the three threes. The sidecards are irrelevant except when two or more players share the three of a kind, when the sidecards do come into play. Thus

beats

as the ace beats the king. Note that subsidiary sidecards can also come into play. For example

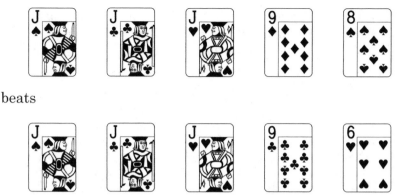

beats

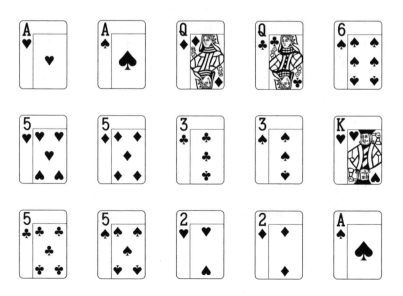

as each side has three jacks with a nine kicker, but the top hand also has an eight which beats the lower hand's six. Again, this is a battle of the kickers.

 NOTE: Three of a kind is also known as *trips*. Thus the above hand is trip jacks.

Two Pair

Ranking just below three of a kind is two pair. A two-pair hand should be self-explanatory and the following are examples:

Again it is the top pair which initially counts if two players both happen to have a two-pair hand. Thus in the hands above the aces and queens beat both the other hands. Meanwhile the fives and threes beat the fives and twos. Kickers can again come into play. For example

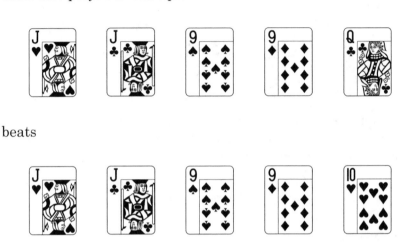

beats

as although both sides have two pair, jacks and nines, the queen beats the ten. Again it is the top pair which is crucial.

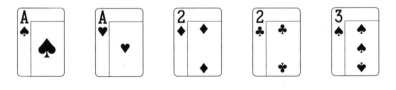

might look a lot more exciting than

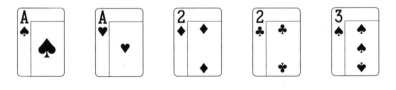

but the harsh fact is that the aces beat the kings.

NOTE: Two-pair hands are often described as *x's up* where 'x' is the higher ranking pair. In the previous example the latter player's aces up beats the former's kings up.

One Pair

A one-pair hand contains just that – one pair with nothing else coordinating. The following are examples:

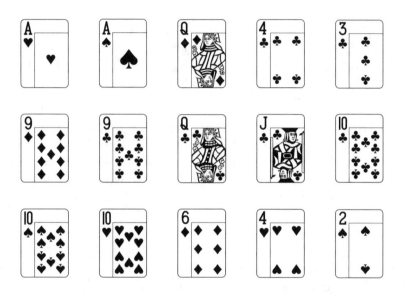

As is to be expected the higher pair wins (the aces in this instance). Note that the middle hand is a very attractive collection with four cards to a straight flush. However, as we know there are no prizes for near misses and the hand is actually just a pair of nines, which is defeated by the final hand of a pair of tens, even though that hand has a motley collection of sidecards compared to those of the nines.

Hands with one pair are where kicker battles can really break out in earnest in hold'em. It is fairly common for one side to share the winning pair, in which case the ranking of the kicker becomes crucial. Here are some examples:

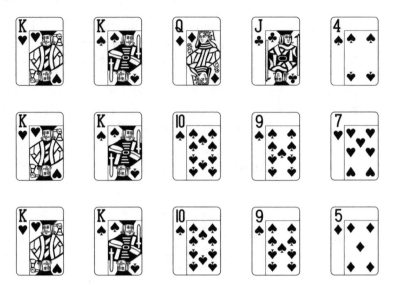

In all cases the players have a pair of kings. The best hand is the top one as the queen kicker beats the ten kickers of the other two hands. To differentiate between the other two hands we have to go down to the third sidecard, when the 7♥ gets the nod over the 5♦.

High Card

If a hand does not come into any of the above categories then it is judged purely on high-card strength. Here are some examples:

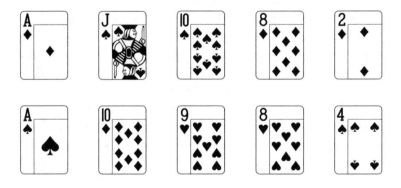

All these hands are ace-high hands. However, the first is ace-jack high, which beats the ace-ten highs of the other two. To find a winner between the other two we must compare the fourth card of each side when we find that the 8♥ wins out against the 7♣.

How Likely?

Note that the hands are ranked in sequence with the least likely hands being ranked higher than the most likely hands. If you were to deal out five cards at random, how likely is it that each of the particular hands will arise? The following table gives the answer.

Hand	Probability
Royal Flush	0.000002
Straight Flush	0.000013
Four of a Kind	0.00024
Full House	0.00144
Flush	0.0020
Straight	0.0039
Three of a Kind	0.0211
Two Pair	0.0475
One Pair	0.4226
High Card	0.5012

As you can see, approximately 92% of random poker hands feature at best one pair.

Exercise One

What are the following hands? (Answers on page 252.)

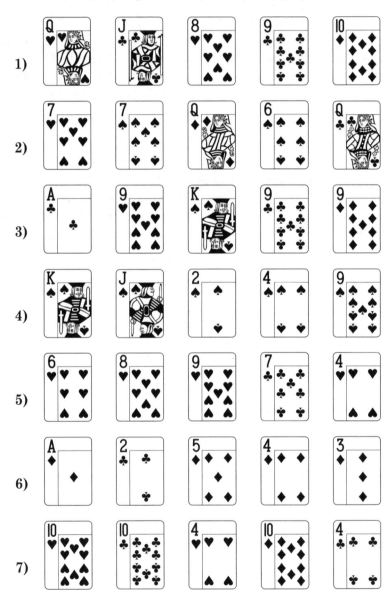

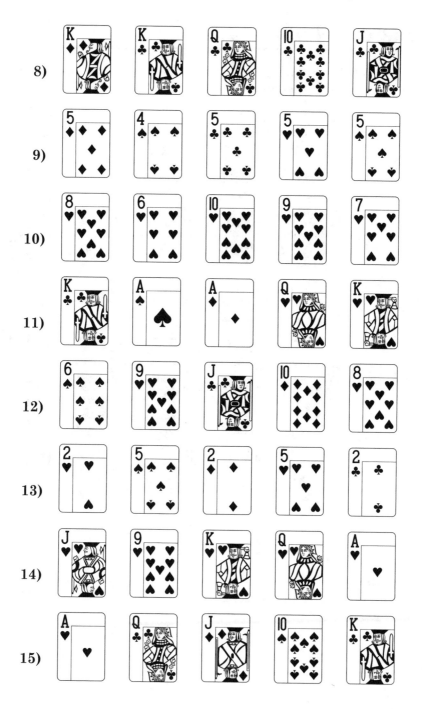

Exercise Two

In each of the following cases there are two hands. Identify the hands and say which one wins. (Answers on page 252.)

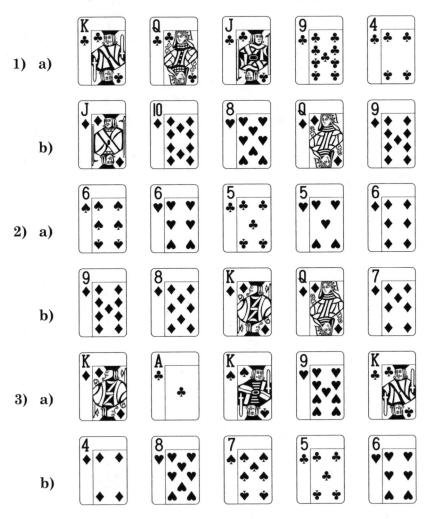

1) a)

b)

2) a)

b)

3) a)

b)

4) a)

b)

5) a)

b)

6) a)

b)

7) a)

b)

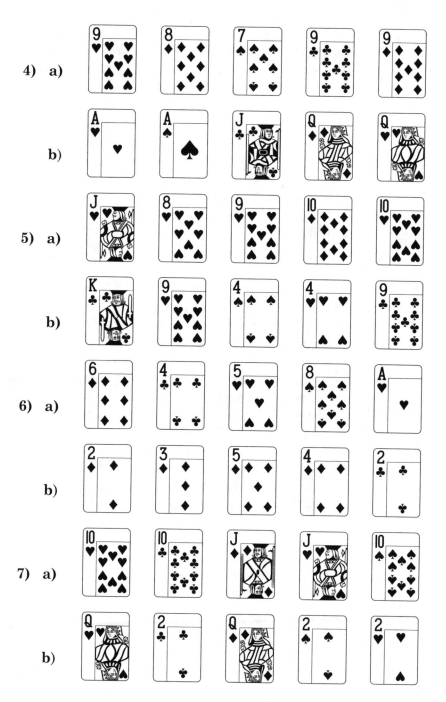

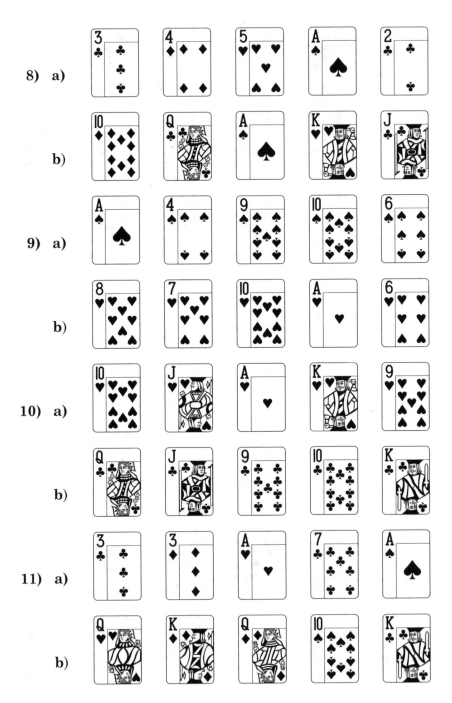

8) a)

b)

9) a)

b)

10) a)

b)

11) a)

b)

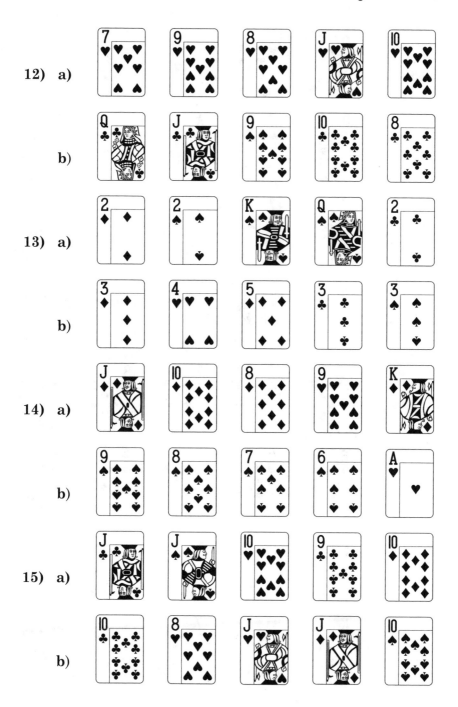

12) a)

b)

13) a)

b)

14) a)

b)

15) a)

b)

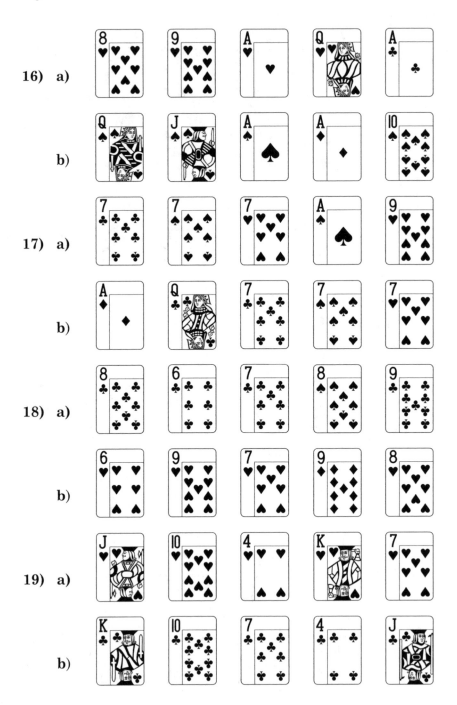

16) a)

b)

17) a)

b)

18) a)

b)

19) a)

b)

Chapter Three

Introducing the Board

- ♣ Using Seven Cards
- ♣ Exercise Three
- ♣ Understanding Hand Strength
- ♣ Exercise Four

Using Seven Cards

A hold'em hand is – at the end of the deal – the best five-card hand you can make from the combination of your own two cards and the five cards on the board. There are 21 possible ways you can combine your two cards with the five board cards to make a hand, and before you can go any further you must become adept at being able to recognise, at a glance, what your hand is.

In the game of Omaha – which can be regarded as a hold'em variant – you get dealt four cards and there are again five board cards for you to combine with and make your best possible hand. However, in Omaha you are obligated to use precisely two of your four cards in combination with the board to make your hand. This is not the case in hold'em. You can use both of your cards, just one of them or – unusually – purely the cards on the table. In this final case you are said to be *playing the board* and this is a rather sad situation to be in as nobody else can possibly have a worse hand than you.

The main things to look for in the seven-card combinations are:

1) Cards of the Same Rank

These cards will make pairs or trips (another way to describe three of a kind) and lead to hands such as two pair, three of a kind or even a full house.

2) Suitedness

If five of your collection are suited, then you have a flush.

3) Connectedness

If five of your collection run in sequence, then you have a straight.

Take a look at the following combinations:

Example 1

The Board

Your Hand

Here your king and jack of hearts combine with the three high hearts on the board to make a royal flush – a fantastic hand.

Example 2

The Board

Your Hand

Your jack and ten of hearts combine with the three hearts on the board to make a straight flush – another wonderful hand.

Example 3

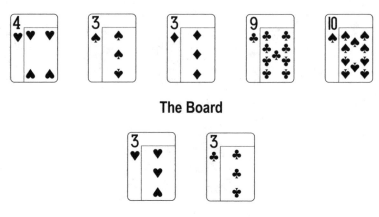

The Board

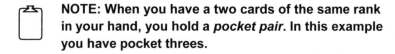

Your Hand

You hold two threes and they match up with the two threes on the board to make four of a kind – yet another major hand.

> **NOTE: When you have a two cards of the same rank in your hand, you hold a *pocket pair*. In this example you have pocket threes.**

Example 4

The Board

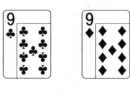

Your Hand

You have a pair of nines (pocket nines) and this is matched by the nine on the board. Combining this three of a kind with the pair of eights on the board generates a full house.

Example 5

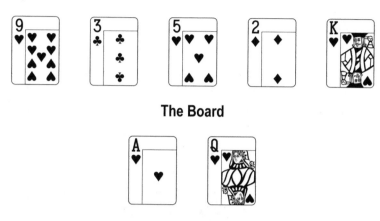

The Board

Your Hand

You have a flush. You have two hearts in your hand and there are three on the board.

Example 6

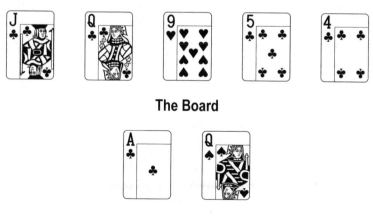

The Board

Your Hand

You have only the A♣, but there are four clubs on the board and this generates your flush. Note that you only need to use your A♣ to make your hand. The Q♠ is irrelevant. An important point is that you hold the best possible missing club. Another player might also have a flush – but you have the best one!

Example 7

The Board

Your Hand

Your J-8 weaves in with the 10-9-7 to form a straight with the sequence J-10-9-8-7.

Example 8

The Board

Your Hand

Again you have a straight. The sequence A-Q-J-10 is on the board, and you can use either of your kings to plug the gap and make a broadway straight. As with Example 6 you will only use one of your cards and, in this particular case, which one you actually use is irrelevant.

Example 9

The Board

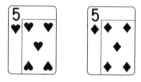

Your Hand

You have a pair of fives and there is a third five on the board. This gives you three of a kind.

Example 10

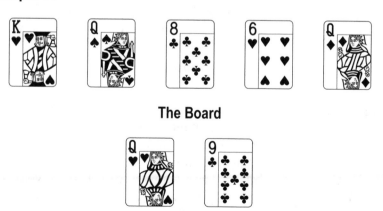

The Board

Your Hand

Here is another way to make three of a kind. This time there is a pair of queens on the board and you have a queen in your hand. Note that in this case you are also using your nine to make your hand because your complete hand is Q-Q-Q-K-9 (your nine outranks the eight and six on the board). This could prove to be important if another player also has a queen in their hand.

 NOTE: When you make a three of a kind hand by using one of your cards to match a pair on the board you have *trips*. Thus, in the above example, you have trip queens. If you have a pair in your hand and this is matched by a card on the board you have a *set*. Thus in Example 9, you hold a set of fives.

Example 11

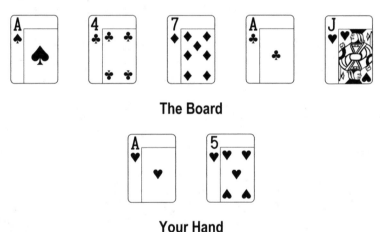

The Board

Your Hand

This example is similar to the previous one, only now your 5♥ 'doesn't play'. Your hand is trip aces – A-A-A-J-7 – you cannot do better than use the board cards for your sidecards. If another player also has an ace in their hand they will beat you if their other card is higher than a seven (or if they have a seven or four which will generate a full house).

Example 12

The Board

Your Hand

Here you have two pair. Your king and jack have both found partners on the board. You have two pairs, kings up.

Example 13

The Board

Your Hand

Here you have just one pair – aces. However, you have a very good sidecard with the queen. If another player has a one pair hand you will only lose to them if they hold precisely A-K. Although this is 'only' a one-pair hand, it is an absolute bread and butter hand at hold'em. I would guess that more hands are won at hold'em by a single pair of aces than by any other holding.

Example 14

The Board

Your Hand

You haven't made anything at all and are stuck with ace high. Nevertheless, it's not a bad ace high – in fact it is the best possible, A-K-Q-J-9. It is not that unusual to win a hold'em hand with just a high card.

Example 15

The Board

Your Hand

You have a two-pair hand – tens and twos. However, everybody else in the hand will also have a two-pair hand if they hold a queen, a nine or a seven (or even a pocket pair). You will have to hope that your opponents are holding either a nine or a seven (making two-pair hands which lose to yours) rather than a queen (making two-pair hands which beat yours).

Example 16

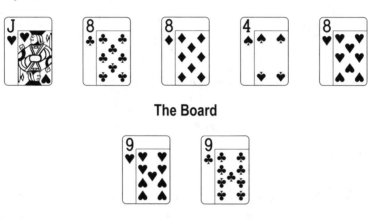

The Board

Your Hand

You have a full house. Your pair of nines combines with the three eights on the board. However, other players are likely to have full houses too. Anyone with a jack in their hand or a higher pocket pair than your nines will make a bigger full house. However, you will beat a player who holds a four. Anyone with the missing eight will be putting on their best poker face.

Exercise Three

What is the best five-card hand in the following combinations? (Answers on page 253.)

Question 1)

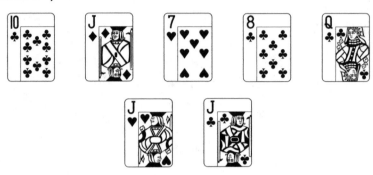

Question 2)

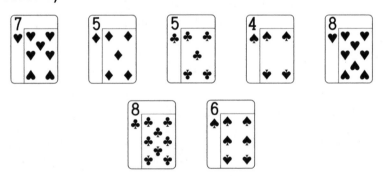

Question 3)

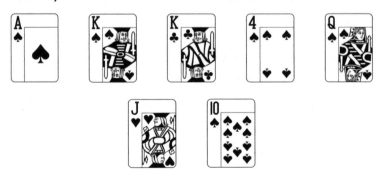

Question 4)

Question 5)

Question 6)

Question 7)

Question 8)

Question 9)

Question 10)

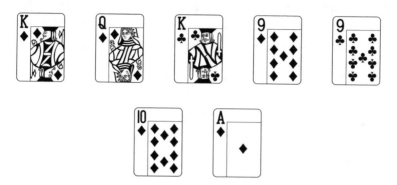

Understanding Hand Strength

If you have looked carefully through the preceding material you should now understand that hands in hold'em are relative. If your poker background comes from playing social games of draw poker or seven-card stud, then it may be difficult to get a handle on this. In draw poker and seven-card stud hands such as flushes and full houses are very strong holdings. In hold'em there are shared board cards and so the value of holdings is relative. We can see this from the following examples:

Example 1a

Here you have a flush. Your 4♣ combines with four clubs on the board to make your flush. So, do you have a good hand?

Well it's not bad but it does not take a great deal to beat you – all someone needs is a higher club. There are plenty of higher clubs out there: 5, 6, 8, 10, J, Q, K – seven in total. Only an opponent with the lowly 3♣ will be paying you off.

Example 1b

Here you again have a flush. Your K♣-J♣ combines with three clubs on the board to make your flush. How strong is your hand now? Very strong. The only way that someone can beat you is if they hold precisely A-x in clubs and, while not impossible, this is not very likely. An opponent with just the bare A♣ has not completed a flush.

Example 2a

Here you have a full house. Your pocket fours combine with the three nines on board to make a full house. A full house is a very big hand. So, how are you doing here? Badly is the answer. It is, again, just too easy for someone to have a better hand. Anyone with a jack or a king has a bigger full house. Anyone with the missing nine (also known as the *case* nine) swamps you with quad nines. Even a player with their own pocket pair will beat you if their pair is higher than your fours.

Example 2b

Here you again have a full house. You have a set of kings and this has combined with the pair of fives on the board to make kings full of fives. This hand – as you might anticipate – is very strong. It is very difficult indeed for someone to have a better hand than you. In fact there is only one way this can happen – if they hold 5-5 for quad fives. This is highly unlikely.

Example 3a

Here you have a two-pair hand: kings and jacks. This is a very modest hand compared with the flush and full house that you held in Examples 1a and 2a. This hand, although much lower in ranking than either of those two, is actually very much stronger. There are no flush or straight possibilities and you hold the best possible two-pair hand. For someone to beat you they will need to have a set, with a pocket pair matching one of the board cards. Such holdings are quite rare.

Example 3b

Here you again have your two-pair hand: kings and jacks. In the previous example we discerned that this was a very powerful holding, so how does this one rate? The answer is very badly indeed – the hand is almost completely useless. There are four hearts on the board as well as the sequence K-Q-J-10. This means that anyone with an ace or a nine beats you with a straight, and anyone with a heart is beating you with a flush. It is highly unlikely that your hand is good.

The key point here is the *texture* of the board. In Example 3a the board was completely uncoordinated. The board in 3b is a different story entirely.

 TIP: When assessing the strength of your holding, a key feature is the *texture* of the board. Moderate holdings such as one or two pair are greatly weakened if the board is coordinated (allowing straight possibilities) or predominantly of one suit (allowing flush possibilities).

Example 4a

Here you have quite a moderate hand – just a pair of kings with a queen kicker. Nevertheless, this is a pretty good holding. You have top pair with the second best possible kicker, and the board is not coordinated at all. With a small number of opponents, it is probable that you have the best hand. The most likely way that you are beaten here is if an opponent has A-K. However, there are a number of plausible holdings for your opponents where you are winning, e.g. K-J, K-10, A-9, 10-9 plus all pocket pairs (barring aces) that have not received help on the board. In all cases your opponent will have a weaker one-pair hand.

Example 4b

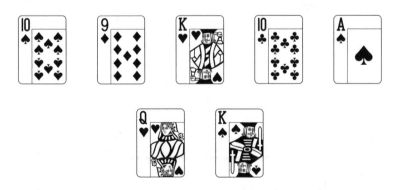

Here again you have your pair of kings. In fact you actually have a two-pair hand – kings and tens – but since the 10-10 is on the board and is shared by everybody, the 'value' of your hand is with the pair of kings. This holding is very much weaker than the one from Example 4a. Here there are two major problems and one small one.

The first major problem is the ace on the board. This means that anyone with just an ace has aces up, beating your kings up. The second big problem is the pair of tens on the board. Anyone with a ten has (at the least) trip tens and this also beats you. A smaller, but nevertheless important, concern is that although you have the best possible kicker with the queen, it doesn't play and your hand is kings and tens with an ace kicker (K-K-10-10-A). This means that anyone else with a king will (at worst) tie with you. Even if they hold K-2, their hand will still be the same as yours.

Having looked through these examples, we can note that there are some key features which help to discern whether a holding is strong or weak:

1) Using Both Cards

It is generally much better if both of your cards are working for you. Whether this is to make a straight, a flush, two pair or even to provide a good kicker, your hand is likely to be much stronger when both cards play.

2) An Opponent needs to use Both Cards to beat You

This is a straightforward corollary to the first point. If an opponent can better you with just a single card (as in Examples 1a, 2a, 3b and 4b) then this is a weakness of your hand. If they must have both cards working for them to beat you (as in Examples 1b, 2b, 3a and 4a) then this strengthens your hand.

3) Coordinating with the Higher/Highest Cards on the Board

A hand that links in with the higher cards on the board is stronger than one that links in with the lower cards. This is seen clearly in Examples 4a and 4b.

The Nuts

The *nuts* is a frequently-used poker term. It simply means the best possible hand with the given board cards. It is not always the most likely hand, and sometimes it is actually rather improbable. However, it is useful to be able to recognise what the nut holding is. Here are some examples:

Example 1

The nut hand is held by anyone with Q-J, generating the top straight.

Example 2

Now with three spades on board the nut hand will be a flush. Thus a player with K-x in spades holds the nuts. Anyone with Q-x in spades holds the *second nuts*.

Example 3

The pair of tens changes everything again as now full houses become possible. The nut hand, however, is quad tens which will be held by anyone lucky enough to have the missing tens. Another very powerful holding is A-A, making the *nut full house* (i.e. other players can hold weaker full houses). This is the second nut hand and would be good enough to win over 99% of the time.

Example 4

At first glance it looks as though there are no straights or flushes available, and so the best hand will be A-A for a set of aces. However, this is actually the second nut hand as 2-4 makes the wheel – the lowest possible straight (5-4-3-2-A).

Summary

The following should be borne in mind when you are 'reading the board':

There is a pair on board

Full houses are possible. Someone could have four of a kind, but this is unusual.

There are no pairs but the board features three or more cards of the same suit

The best possible hand is a flush. There is an exception – if the flush cards are coordinated then a straight flush becomes possible.

There are no pairs and no flush possibilities

If there are three cards sufficiently close together in rank then a straight is possible. Otherwise a set is the best possible hand.

Exercise Four

In each of the following cases your cards are given along with the board cards. For each example, you must answer the following questions:

a) What is your hand?

b) What hands beat you?

(Answers on page 254.)

 NOTE: This is purely an exercise in hand recognition and board reading. Just because theoretically stronger hands are possible does not mean that opponents will definitely hold them or are even likely to.

Question 1)

Question 2)

Question 3)

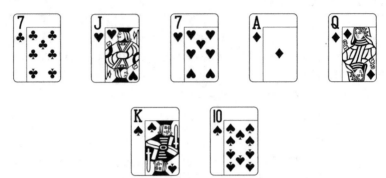

Question 4)

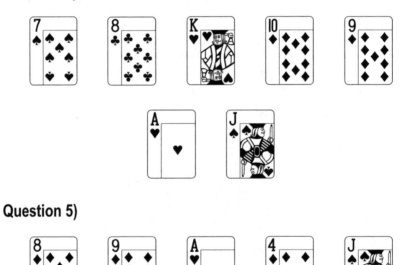

Question 5)

Question 6)

Question 7)

Question 8)

In each of the following cases your cards are given along with the board cards, but there is one further card still to be dealt. In each case, answer the questions:

a) Which cards will improve your hand?

b) Which of these cards will give you the nuts?

In both cases you can assume that by 'improve' you have to improve to a better hand than just a single pair.

(Answers on page 254.)

Question 9)

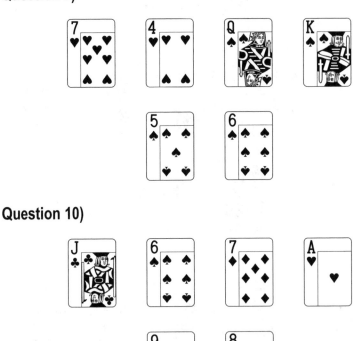

Question 10)

Chapter Four

The Basics of Play

- ♣ **How Limit Hold'em is Played**
- ♣ **The Betting**
- ♣ **A Practical Example**
- ♣ **Exercise Five**
- ♣ **Other Forms of Poker**

How Limit Hold'em is Played

Limit hold'em can be played with any number of players between two (heads-up) or ten (a full ring game). Most games are played with between eight and ten players at the table. Many players like to play short-handed games (typically featuring between four and six players) but this requires rather specialised skills and is not recommended for beginners. Other players like to play heads-up with just two players at the table. Such encounters can be great fun (and also profitable for a skilled player) but their dynamics are so different from full ring play that they almost constitute a completely different game. For the purposes of this introductory material I am going to discuss how play operates in a full ring game.

The players sitting at various positions around the table can be identified by their positions. These terms are in very common usage in poker literature and it is good to get used to them as soon as possible. Here is a table featuring ten players:

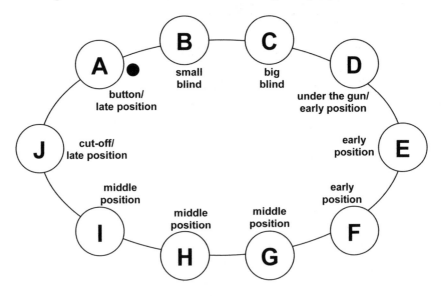

Table Positions

The first player is Alan and he has a 'button' in front of him to signify that he is, in principle, the dealer. In live play such as in a casino, the dealer would actually have a small round object, the button, placed in front of him, to signify his status. In online play this is represented graphically by a small on-screen blob. Alan will remain the dealer throughout the hand, regardless of whether he is still in the pot or not.

The next player to consider is the one to the button's immediate left. This position is the small blind and in our example here this spot is occupied by Belinda. Next comes Charlie who finds himself in the spot known as the big blind.

To the immediate left of the big blind is the position known as the under-the-gun (UTG). In our table above this position is held by Donna. Donna, along with Edward and Fiona who are to her immediate left, are known as early position players.

The next three players, Gary, Heather and Ian are all middle position players. The player sitting to Ian's immediate left is Julie, who is in the cut-off seat. Julie and Alan, who is the dealer, are collectively known as late position players.

The position of the button rotates clockwise around the table. Thus on this hand Alan has the button but on the next deal it will move to Belinda when Charlie and Donna will find themselves in the small and big blinds respectively. After Belinda, it will be Charlie's turn to deal and so on.

The Blinds

There has to be something in the pot at the start of play, otherwise there is nothing to fight for. In hold'em this is handled by having two *blinds*: a small blind and a big blind. These players are obligated to put money into the pot at the start of the hand. The small blind puts up a sum (typically) equivalent to half of a small bet and the big blind contributes a small bet. Thus in a $1-$2 game, the small blind is $0.50 and the big blind is $1, whilst in a $20-$40 game the sums are $10 and $20 respectively.

At some limits there is no simple way to halve the small blind. This is how three of these limits are usually dealt with:

Game	Small Blind
$3-$6 game	$1
$5-$10 game	$2
$15-$30 game	$10

Note the slight illogicallity in that in the $3-$6 game the small blind is one-third of the big blind, whereas in the $15-$30 game it is two-thirds.

The Play of the Hand

After the blind money has been put in the pot each player is dealt two cards – their hand. There is now a round of betting known as the pre-flop betting round. The unit for this betting round is a small bet. Thus in a $5-$10 game players will bet in units of $5. Players who like the look of their cards will be betting and raising, whilst players with unfavourable cards will be folding (also known as *mucking*). Players who fold their cards are out and will play no further part in the hand. We will discuss the betting at greater length very shortly.

The pre-flop betting round is unusual in that the first player to 'speak' is the UTG. On all subsequent rounds the first player to speak will be the small blind. After the UTG player has acted, play moves clockwise around the table.

After the pre-flop betting is completed, three cards are dealt face up in the centre of the table. These three cards are known collectively as the *flop* and we now have the flop betting round. If the small blind is still in the pot (he may, of course, have folded during the pre-flop round of betting) then he will be the first to speak, followed by the big blind, the UTG and so on. The unit for the flop betting round is again one small bet.

Once the flop betting is completed, a single card is dealt to join the other three communal cards on the table. This card is known as the *turn* and after it has been dealt we have the turn betting. Again the small blind is first to speak. The unit for the turn betting round is one big bet – double the size of the pre-flop and flop rounds.

At the conclusion of the turn betting, a final card is dealt to join the other four in the middle. This is the *river* card and we now have the river betting. The unit for the river betting is again one big bet. All cards have now been dealt. When the river betting is complete players who are still in the pot show down their hands and the best hand takes the pot.

> **NOTE: There are four rounds of betting: pre-flop, flop, turn and river.**

Betting Round	Bet Size	In a $5-$10 game
Pre-flop	Big Blind	$5
Flop	Big Blind	$5
Turn	2 x Big Blind	$10
River	2 x Big Blind	$10

The Betting

In limit hold'em the amount you can bet (or raise) at any point is fixed. A round of betting is completed when all players who are still active in the hand have contributed the same amount of money to the pot.

Responding to a Bet

When the action comes to you and there has already been a bet – or a bet and one or more raises – then there are three options:

1) You can fold

Maybe you do not like the look of your hand or maybe you regard the amount of money that you need to put into the pot to stay active in the hand as too much. In that case, you can simply throw your hand away. You contribute no money to the pot and your participation in the hand is over.

2) You can call

Perhaps you have a middling hand. It might seem too good to throw away just yet, but maybe you are not sure where you stand. Now a good option is to *call* the bet. To do this you have to place an amount of money in the pot which matches the current level of the bet. Thus, if the current unit of the betting round is $5 and there has just been a bet (and maybe one or more calls), then you can call for $5. If there has already been a bet and a raise, then it will cost $10 to call.

3) You can raise

Maybe you like the look of your hand and suspect that you have the best chance to win the pot. Now you want to take the initiative and make the other players pay extra to stay with you – and so you raise. To do this you match the current bet and then add one extra betting unit for the raise. So, if there has just been a bet on a $5 round, then to raise you will put $10 into the pot. Now anyone who has only put $5 in so far will have to call your raise if they wish to continue.

Acting when there is no Bet

Sometimes on a betting round it happens that when the action comes to you, no-one else has yet bet anything. Now you have two options:

1) You can check

You do not put any money into the pot but you remain in the hand. Of course, someone may now bet subsequent to you and then you will be forced to (at least) call the bet if you wish to stay active in the pot. Sometimes, however, everybody checks and no money enters the pot on that particular betting round.

2) You can bet

You put the equivalent of one betting unit into the pot and oblige other players to (at least) call your bet if they wish to continue in the pot.

Note that it is not possible (for players not in the big blind) to check on the pre-flop betting round, as it is necessary to call the forced bet from the big blind. Thus no-one (excepting the big blind) can get to see the flop cards without committing some money to the pot.

Further Notes on Betting

1) Keeping the Betting Open

Whenever a player raises they are keeping the betting open. Every other player who is still in the pot will have to call the raise, and this will give them the opportunity to re-raise if they wish.

2) Closing the Betting

At some point there will be only one player remaining who has not yet called the bet. If this player does call (rather than raising) then the betting is *closed* and play moves on to the next round. Note that if this player were to fold the effect would be the same – every player remaining in the pot would have called the bet and play would again move on to the next round.

3) Capping the Betting

Raising and re-raising cannot go on indefinitely. In online games (this can vary slightly in live-action play) it is standard for the betting to be *capped* by the third raise. Thus if there is a bet, a raise and a re-raise then only one further raise is possible. The player making this final raise is said to be capping the pot. Thus on a $5 betting round the maximum that each player can contribute to the pot is $20 (a bet and three raises). If the action comes to you and the pot has already been capped, then you cannot raise. Your choices are limited to calling the bet or folding.

4) When Everyone Folds

If one player decides to bet or raise during the course of a betting round and everybody else folds, then the pot is immediately won by that player, regardless of their cards.

This may all sound terribly complicated, but it is actually quite straightforward and you will soon get the hang of it. Let's see how it works in practice.

A Practical Example

In this example we will consider a $5-$10 game, featuring our previous crowd of players. We will not be overly concerned about the quality of the play and whether the players are making good or bad decisions. This section is purely to give an example of the mechanics of play.

Pre-Flop Play

Before any cards have been dealt the small blind will contribute $2 to the pot and the big blind $5. Thus the pot stands at $7. Now the cards are dealt and the big blind (Charlie) is considered to have made a bet (in fact this is a *forced* bet) of $5 and it is now up to the UTG (Donna) to respond. The players (indicated by initials) and their cards are as given below:

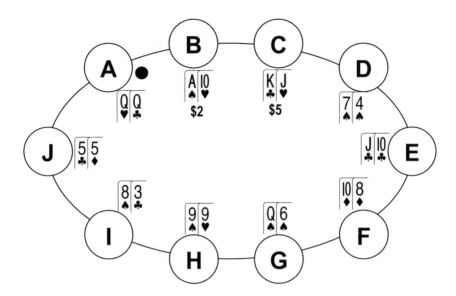

As we saw before Donna now has the three options: folding, calling or raising. As it is Donna has a feeble holding and decides – sensibly – to save her money for later battles. She folds.

Play now passes round to Edward who has exactly the same options as Donna. Edward has two moderately high cards which have the additional benefit of being suited (good for flushes) and connected (good for straights). This is a reasonable hand, but Edward does not want to get carried away just yet. He decides to call the $5 forced bet from Charlie.

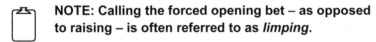 **NOTE: Calling the forced opening bet – as opposed to raising – is often referred to as *limping*.**

The pot now stands at $12. Fiona, like Edward, has cards that are useful for straights and flushes, but nevertheless, 10-8 is quite a weak holding and she decides to fold. Gary's Q-6 is a poor hand and he also folds.

Play now moves on to Heather. Heather has a medium strength pair which is a fairly decent holding. She likes the look of her hand and decides to raise. She thus puts $10 into the pot, bringing it to $22. The situation is now as given below:

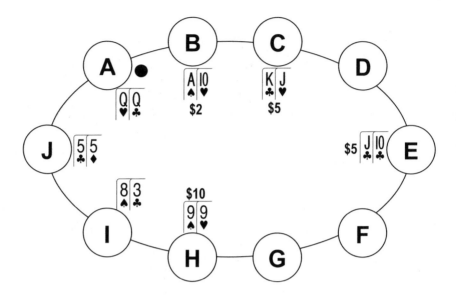

Note that the money that has been bet so far on this round has not actually yet gone into the pot. This will only happen when the current round of betting is complete.

Ian has junk cards and folds, but Julie likes the look of her small pair and calls the bet – which is now $10, following the earlier raise from Heather. The pot increases to $32.

It is now Alan's turn. Alan's pair of queens is a premium holding. The only hands which are better than this are A-A and K-K. Alan likes the look of his hand so much that he wants to re-raise and get as much money into the pot as possible. First of all, he has to match the existing bet of $10 and then add an extra $5 for the raise. He thus bets a total of $15 and the pot is up to $47.

Belinda considers for a moment. She has already been obliged (by virtue of being in the small blind) to put $2 into the pot. If she wants to continue playing the hand she must now put an additional $13 into the pot in order to call Alan's $15 bet. If she is feeling particularly aggressive she could raise too. She would achieve this by matching the $13 and raising a further $5. However, although her A-10 is a decent hand, she has already seen a bet, a raise and a re-raise. In these circumstances she realises that there will be some very decent hands out against her and she folds her hand. Charlie in the big blind has a similar decision to make. However, he has already 'bet' (by being the big blind) $5 and so it is only $10 for him to call. His hand, with two face cards, is not bad and he decides that, as he is getting a 'cheap' call he will come along for the ride. He adds a further $10 to the existing $5 to call the $15 bet from Alan. Note that everyone has now had a chance to contribute to the betting. Some players have folded, some have called, Heather has raised and Alan has re-raised. The situation is now as follows.

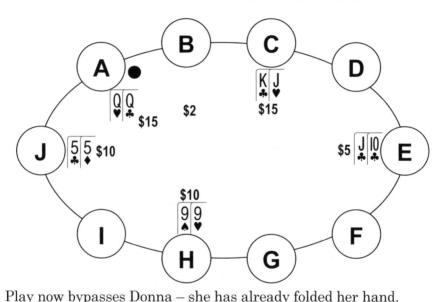

Play now bypasses Donna – she has already folded her hand. Edward originally put $5 in the pot and must now add a further $10 if he wishes to call or $15 if he decides to raise. He decides to call and adds a further $10 to the pot bringing it up to $67.

The action now passes to Heather. Remember that she originally raised and so has already committed $10 to the pot. She also calls the extra $5 and the pot is now at $72. Julie has a similar decision and she also calls. This costs her $5 too and the pot now stands at $77. Note that everybody who is still in the pot has now bet exactly $15 in this round of betting. Julie's call has closed the betting and the pre-flop play is now complete. There are five players remaining in the pot: Alan, Charlie, Edward, Heather and Julie. They have all contributed $15 to the pot and Belinda has contributed $2, although she is no longer active in the pot. Her $2 is known as *dead* money.

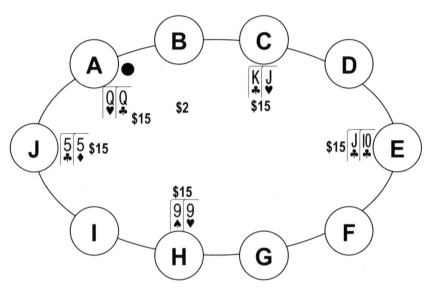

Now that the pre-flop betting round is complete, the bets are swept up into the central pot and the flop cards are dealt.

There are five players left in and the pot stands at $77.

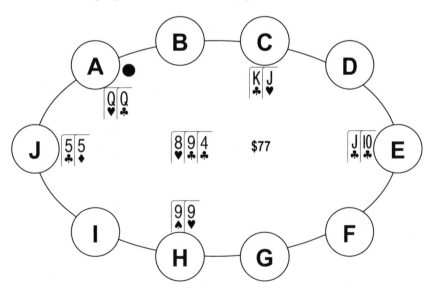

Flop Play

On the previous round the first person to speak was the UTG player – Donna. Now – and on all subsequent rounds – the first player to speak will be Belinda, the small blind. Here, however, Belinda has already folded and so play passes directly to Charlie in the big blind. As there has not yet been a bet, Charlie now has different options. In fact, he is not obligated to bet anything at all – he can instead check. This means that he puts no money into the pot at all and play would pass to Edward. Charlie sees that the flop has not helped his hand in any way whatsoever – he has no pairs and no chances to make any straights or flushes. He checks.

Edward, unlike Charlie, has received considerable help from the flop. Although he has not made any pairs he can combine his J-10 with the 9-8 on the flop to form the running sequence J-10-9-8. If he is lucky and either a queen or a seven comes on the later rounds, he will have made a straight. However, there is yet more good news. He also has two clubs in his hand which match the two clubs on the flop. Therefore a further club on the flop will give him a flush. Although Edward does not actually have a *made* hand at the moment (he currently holds a mere jack high), he has tremendous potential. He has a good chance to make either a straight or a flush, and if he does, he will be in great shape. These holdings can only be beaten by a full house or better (or a higher straight or flush) and such hands are very hard to make. Despite the fact that his hand has excellent potential, Edward is a cautious player and he decides to check. Play now passes to Heather.

Heather, who was the original raiser on the pre-flop round, is thrilled by the flop. Whenever you hold a pair and the third card arrives on board to match your pair and give you three of a kind, you are in a very strong position. In order to beat your three of a kind, a player will need to make at least a straight, a flush or a higher three of a kind. Even if an opponent improves to a straight or flush (and it is unlikely) you still have a chance to improve your three of a kind to a full house (or even quads) and overtake them.

Because Heather has such a strong hand you might expect her to bet, but in fact she doesn't. Instead she checks. As we shall see, this is part of a plan to exploit her excellent hand to the full.

Julie has a pair of fives and is disappointed that a further five has not appeared to make her three of a kind. She realises that she is not in good shape. If anyone started the hand with a higher pair than her then they will still have a better hand. Meanwhile if another player started with a hand that contained either a nine or an eight then they will now have made a higher pair than her fives. With four opponents, she realises that it is probable that someone is doing better than her and she also checks.

Alan now considers how the flop has helped his hand and likes what he sees. His pair of queens is higher than any card on the flop, so even if someone has a nine or an eight in their hand, he is still ahead. He is pleased that no aces or kings have appeared on the flop, as these would have given someone a chance to overtake him by making a higher pair. This is actually a very good flop for Alan (he is not to know of course about the monster hand that Heather holds) and he decides to bet $5.

As we saw earlier the flop has done nothing for Charlie's prospects, and he sensibly decides to abandon ship and folds. As we know, Edward has an excellent drawing hand and he has little hesitation in calling the $5 bet. The situation is now as follows:

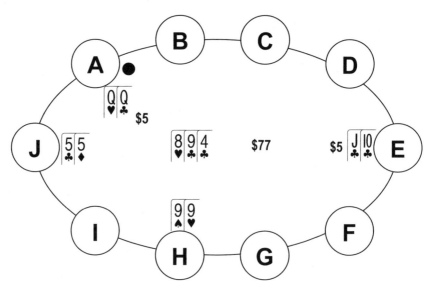

Play passes to Heather who reveals the strength of her hand with a raise. As her initial action on this round was a check, her subsequent raise is known as a *check-raise*. Had she originally bet then it is possible that there would not have been any raises and that anybody who wanted to stay in the hand would have only had to put in $5. Now, however, anyone who wants to stay in will have to contribute (at least) $10 on this round. Heather has a very strong hand and she wants to get as much money into the pot as possible. Her check-raise is a clever way of doing this. Play passes to Julie.

Even before the betting started on this round Julie realised that her pair of fives was unlikely to be a good hand here, and the subsequent action has convinced her of this. She folds.

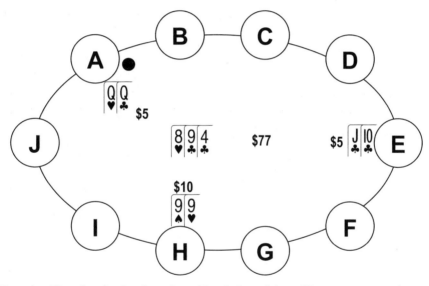

Despite Heather's check-raise, Alan's hand is still very strong. As far as he knows, Heather might have just a single nine or eight (making one pair) and think that she is winning. He knows that his hand is better and he now re-raises, putting an extra $10 in and bringing the bet for the current round up to $15.

Edward is slightly taken aback by all this raising but, as we know, his hand has tremendous potential and he calls the re-raise, putting a further $10 into the pot.

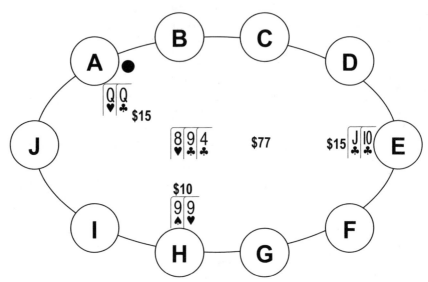

Heather is delighted. She has the best hand right now and she raises yet again, placing a further $10 into the pot and increasing the bet to $20. This is the third raise and no more raises are possible. The betting is said to be *capped*. The only options available to Alan and Edward are now to call or fold.

It costs both of them $5 to stay in the pot and they both call.

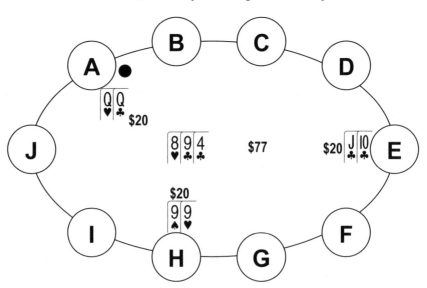

The flop betting is now complete, the bets are swept up into the pot and the turn card is dealt.

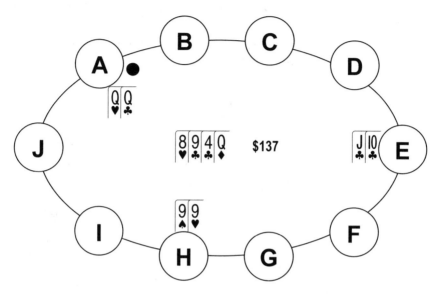

Turn Play

The pre-flop and flop play is complete and now – for the turn and river rounds – the betting unit doubles to $10. It is now Edward's turn to speak as he is now the first remaining active player in the pot as we move clockwise round the table from the dealer. Edward is thrilled. A queen has arrived to complete his straight. Now Edward hatches the same plan as that used by Heather on the previous round. So far in this hand it has been Heather and Alan who have done all the raising and re-raising, whereas Edward has been meekly calling along. He realises that no-one will suspect that he now has such a strong hand and so he checks, assuming that one of his opponents will bet and he can then check-raise.

Play passes to Heather. Although she had a hugely powerful hand on the flop, this queen has now enabled both her opponents to overtake her. We know that Edward has made a straight, and Alan now has a higher three of a kind. Heather, of course, doesn't know any of this. She still has a very good hand and sees no reason not to bet $10.

Alan, like Edward, is thrilled by the turn card and he quickly raises, betting $20. Much to the surprise of Heather and Alan, the previously quiet Edward now leaps in with a re-raise, bumping the bet up to $30.

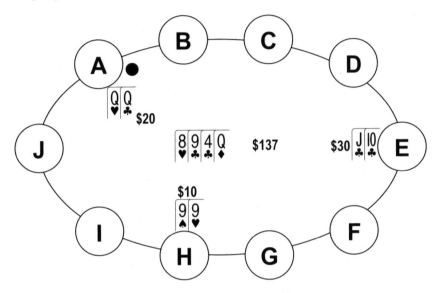

For the first time in the hand, Heather is now concerned that her wonderful three of a kind might not be the best hand after all. She realises that if Edward is holding J-10 then he has made a straight. She cannot be certain that this is what he has, but he has made an extremely aggressive play and she (correctly) suspects the worst. Nevertheless, she is not without hope. If a pair appears on the board with the river card then she will improve to a full house and overtake Edward's straight. She calls the $20.

Alan reasons the hand out the same way as Heather and also suspects that Edward has made a straight. He calls and also hopes to make a full house on the river. The bets are swept up and the river card comes down.

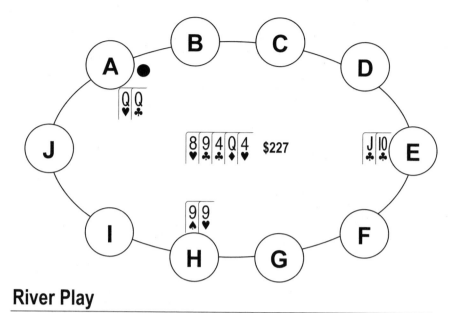

River Play

Finally the river card is dealt. Heather and Alan are both delighted as they have now improved their three of a kind hands to full houses and realise that they will have overtaken Edward if he had a straight.

It is again Edward's turn to open the betting. He is a little concerned by the river card, as he realises that it is possible one of his opponents now has a full house (it is not possible for a player to have a full house without there being, at the very least, one pair on the board). Nevertheless, he decides to bet and his worst fears are confirmed when Heather raises.

Alan can't believe his luck. He has the big full house and there has been a bet and a raise before him. Naturally he re-raises.

Edward realises that the game is almost certainly up. Nevertheless this pot is so big that he does not want to make a horrible mistake by folding the best hand and so he makes a *crying call* for $20. Heather suspects the worst and also calls.

Alan wins the pot – his queens full of fours beating Heather's nines full of fours and Edward's straight. He takes down a huge $317 pot.

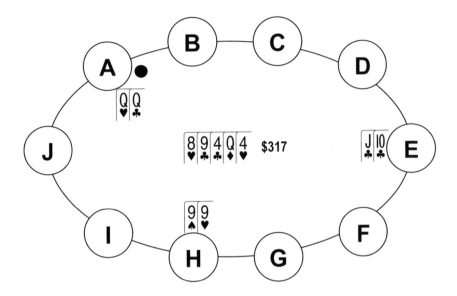

Heather and Edward were rather unlucky. Heather in particular had a fabulous hand, and it was very unfortunate for her that she happened to be up against a monster. Sadly hold'em is a winner-takes-it-all game, and there are no prizes for having an excellent runner-up hand.

This was an action-packed example with bets, raises and re-raises on every street. Very few hold'em hands see anywhere near this much action. A typical size for a hold'em pot is approximately 5-6 times the big bet. Thus in a $5-$10 game one would expect an average pot to be about $50-$60. A pot of $317 is thus gigantic.

The Rake

You will not be surprised to learn that online poker sites make an awful lot of money, which is why they attract valuations of millions and even billions of dollars. The way they make their money is exactly the same as the way casinos and cardrooms make their money from poker – they take a *rake* out of each pot. The rake is the site's fee for managing the games and it is typically between $1 and $3 per pot, depending upon the final pot size. A typical rake might be as follows: $1 for a pot smaller than $30, $2 for a pot between $30 and $50 and $3 for a pot over $50. Sometimes the rake is capped at, say, $2 if the game has six players or less. Also, sites usually have a 'no flop, no drop' policy meaning that if a hand is concluded pre-flop (with every player bar one folding) then no rake is deducted from the pot. I have not deducted a house rake from the pot in the above example, but it would probably be $3 and Alan would thus take $314 from the pot rather than $317.

Exercise Five

(Answers on page 255).

1) In a $10-$20 game how much is the small blind?

2) In a $3-$6 game how much is the big blind?

3) Who sits on the immediate left of the dealer?

4) Who is last to speak on the pre-flop betting round?

5) In a $1-$2 game how much is the betting unit on the flop round?

6) In a $50-$100 game how much is the betting unit on the turn round?

7) You are sitting in middle position in a $10-$20 game. An early player opens with a raise and the action comes round to you. If you want to raise, how much money must you bet?

8) Who (assuming they are still in the pot) is first to speak on all rounds except the pre-flop round?

9) In a $10-$20 game an early player calls and everyone folds round to the small blind. How much must the small blind put in to call?

10) After an initial bet, how many raises can there be before the betting is capped?

Other Forms of Poker

Congratulations. You now know how to play limit hold'em. However, there are many variants of poker and you may be curious as to how the major ones operate. Here is a brief summary of the other forms.

No-Limit Hold'em

The other way to play hold'em is to play no-limit. In no-limit hold'em a player can bet any amount of money at any time. This makes the game much more dangerous than limit as your entire stack is vulnerable any time you enter a pot. The structure of play though, is really the same as for limit hold'em with all the rules regarding checking, betting, raising etc, still applying. However, you can bet any amount and you can raise any amount.

There is no compelling reason why hold'em should not be played at pot-limit, but this version is quite rare. The limit and no-limit forms dominate.

Tournament Hold'em

The majority of major poker events (including the prestigious World Series of Poker) feature no-limit hold'em. In tournaments each competitor begins with the same amount of chips. The play is just as for a normal no-limit hold'em game, except that if you lose your stack you are eliminated from the event.

Play is speeded up by increasing the levels of the blinds at regular intervals. At the start of play the blinds may be a tiny fraction of the chip stacks, and players can survive simply by being extremely conservative. However, towards the end of the event, the blinds have usually increased substantially and can represent significant percentages of players' stacks. When this happens (or when it becomes likely to happen) players can no longer sit around passively, or they will be *blinded away*.

Tournaments can vary enormously in the number of players competing. Small online tournaments are often played on just one table and are called *sit'n'go's*. They start with just ten players and usually take less than an hour to complete. Larger events are played multi-table and, as players are eliminated, tables are merged to keep each table as full as possible. Small online events regularly start with 20 or 30 players while bigger ones might start with a few hundred. Such events can last for several hours. Major live tournaments such as the World Series of Poker often see starting line-ups of a thousand or more players and these events can run over several days.

Tournaments pay out the top places on a sliding scale. For example, a sit'n'go featuring ten players with an entry fee of $10 (plus a little extra for the cardroom's registration fees) has $100 available in prize money. This is usually split with $50 to the winner, $30 to the runner-up and $20 to the player coming third. Bigger tournaments can provide huge prizes for the players making it down to the final three or four places.

Omaha

Omaha is a different game from hold'em, although there are considerable similarities. Each player receives four cards rather than two and the board comprises of five cards as with hold'em. An important rule in Omaha is that you must use precisely two of your cards to make a hand. For players used to playing hold'em, this can be very confusing at first. For example, if you have A♣-K♥-9♦-9♠ and the board shows J♣-3♣-6♣-Q♦-4♣ you might think that you have a flush. In fact you don't, as you have only the bare A♣ and no accompanying club in your hand. Change your hand to A♣-K♥-9♦-9♣ and now you really do have a flush.

As players get four cards, the hands that can be made are very much stronger than in hold'em. Hands that win pots are generally straights, flushes and full houses. It is quite common for a player to hold the nut hand in Omaha, whereas this is rather rare in hold'em.

The structure of play in Omaha is the same as for hold'em, but the game is nearly always played in pot-limit format. For various technical reasons, it does not make much sense as a game at no-limit or limit. It is perfectly possible to play tournament

Omaha and this is quite popular. Again this is played pot-limit.

Omaha Eight or Better

Omaha eight or better is a *split-pot* game and again the stipulation of using precisely two cards is in place. At the end of play the pot is split between the best high hand (normal poker rules apply) and the best low hand. The best low hand is the wheel (5-4-3-2-A) with the next best being 6-4-3-2-A.

In order to qualify for the low half of the pot, you must have a hand that is no worse than eight-low (hence Omaha eight or better). This means that unless the board features three cards of different rank below nine, it is impossible to make a low hand and the winning high hand will scoop the entire pot. Thus if the board is A-5-9-6-K you *can* make a low hand (the nut low in this case would be held by a player holding 2-3). However, boards such as K-Q-7-4-9 and J-6-6-2-2 do not permit low hands.

Omaha eight or better is usually played limit or pot-limit and tournaments based on Omaha eight or better are also popular.

Chapter Five

How Hands Develop

- ♣ **Starting Hands – Basic Principles**
- ♣ **The Concept of Outs**
- ♣ **Playing Hands**
- ♣ **Focusing on Outs**
- ♣ **Exercise Six**
- ♣ **Developing a Feel**

We have already practised the job of extracting our best five-card hand from the seven cards that are on the board after the final river card has been dealt. Now, however, we need to concentrate on how hands develop from the pre-flop stage through the flop, turn and river.

For the moment we will not worry about the betting – we are just going to see how hands can develop and specifically look at how worse hands can overtake better hands with helpful cards on the turn and/or river.

Before we examine closely how hands develop, I want to briefly introduce two other elements of hold'em: starting hands and the concept of outs.

Starting Hands – Basic Principles

At this point I want to say a few words about starting hands (there will be very much more to say about this later).

When you play hold'em in a full ring game you should normally adopt a fairly *tight* style of play. This means that you will probably only play about 20-25% of the hands that you are dealt. The others will be so poor that you will discard them at the pre-flop stage. So, what sort of hands will you play and why?

There are the three basic types of hand which you should look for opportunities to play:

1) Pairs

A-A is the best possible starting hand, but all big pairs (K-K, Q-Q, J-J and 10-10) are very good holdings. These hands can often win pots without improving. Medium pairs (9-9, 8-8 and 7-7) are often playable but not always. They will occasionally win pots without improving. Small pairs (sixes down to twos) will rarely win pots without improving, but are nevertheless playable in the right conditions.

2) High Cards

The best high card combination is A-K. Other good high card holdings are A-Q, A-J, K-Q, K-J and Q-J. If they are suited (creating flush possibilities) then that is a bonus, but high card combinations are often playable purely on their high card strength. You are basically hoping to make a big pair on the flop, when there is a good chance you have the best hand. Additionally, you will occasionally have possibilities to make straights and flushes (assuming you are suited).

3) Suited Connectors

These are suited cards, adjacent in rank, e.g. 9♣-8♣, 5♥-4♥, 10♦-9♦. By playing these hands you are hoping to get a favourable flop which gives you chances to make straights and flushes. These are speculative hands – much of the time the flop will be bad for you and you will have to give up.

Before we look at the hands I want to introduce a common poker terms which is of great use here – outs.

The Concept of Outs

At any stage in a hand of hold'em one player will have the best hand but the opposition will (almost always) have chances to improve significantly. The cards that help them to improve are called *outs*. Generally this is taken to mean cards that can improve your hand in such a way that your hand is now likely to overtake a previously better one.

Here is an example:

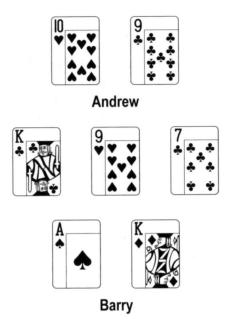

Andrew

Barry

Barry is playing a strong starting hand with the best possible non-pair hand, A-K. Andrew has a weaker holding with two lower cards. Barry is, of course, favourite, but all that can easily change as cards arrive on the board, and the values of the players' hands can alter dramatically.

Once the flop has been dealt, both sides find that they have a pair. Barry is currently ahead because his pair of kings beats Andrew's pair of nines. In order to improve and overtake Barry, Andrew will need to hit one of his outs. So, what are his outs?

Firstly notice that (for the moment at least) Andrew has no straight or flush possibilities. The only way he can overtake Barry is by improving to a two-pair or three of a kind hand. The cards that will help him are nines (to generate three of a kind) or tens (to make two pair). The situation below shows a nine arriving on the turn:

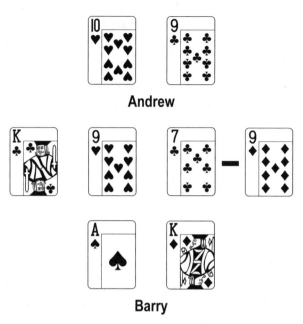

Andrew

Barry

Andrew now has three of a kind and is beating Barry. A ten will also do the trick:

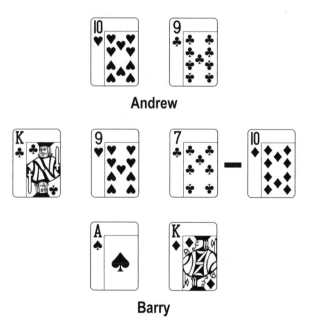

Andrew

Barry

Andrew now has two pair and is again beating Barry.

Thus, on the flop, Andrew has three tens and two nines which improve him to a winning hand. He has precisely five outs.

But what about if a seven appears on the turn? The situation is now as follows:

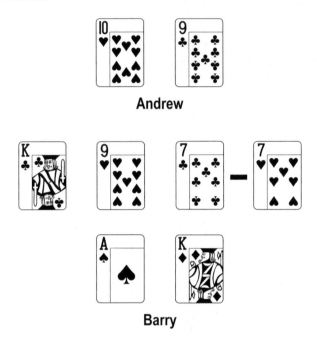

Andrew

Barry

Andrew now has two pairs, nines and sevens. So does this mean he has overtaken Barry? No! The pair of sevens is on the board, and thus Barry can also use them to make a two-pair hand. His kings and sevens still beats Andrew's nines and sevens. The second pair is shared and thus does not benefit either player (any other player who happened to have a seven in his hand *would* benefit, of course). The players both improve from a one-pair hand to a two-pair hand and Barry retains the lead thanks to his higher pair.

This can continue on the river. If the river card is yet another seven we then have the following situation:

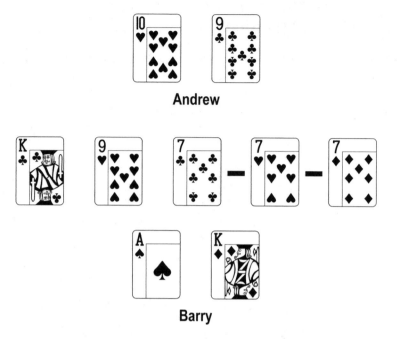

Andrew

Barry

Andrew has improved yet again – he now has a full house, sevens over nines. The turn and river cards have improved his hand from one pair to two pair to a full house. Unfortunately, this 'improvement' has all been in vain as Barry has improved in a similar way and now holds a full house sevens over kings and is winning.

This demonstrates two important principles in hold'em.

Better Hands often remain Better

Hands that are better on the flop often remain so all the way through to the river, even though the hands improve in their rankings.

Holdings are Relative

Having a high ranking hand in hold'em is of limited use if it is very easy for other players to have high ranking hands too.

Hands with Potential

It is quite common for cards to appear on the turn which do not immediately help either hand, but create further potential for improvement. Let's rewind back to the flop situation and imagine that the turn card is the 8♣. The situation is now as follows.

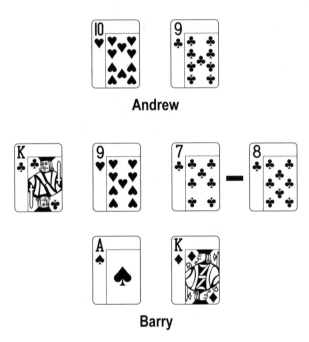

Andrew

Barry

This card has not improved either player's hand and Barry's pair of kings is still beating Andrew's pair of nines. However, it has given Andrew tremendous potential for two reasons:

> 1) There are now three clubs on the board and he has a club in his hand. Any further club on the river will complete a flush for him.
>
> 2) He has a ten in his hand which, allied with the sequence 9-8-7 on the board creates the chance to make a straight. Any jack or six will complete this straight.

Previously Andrew had only five outs, but this turn card has hugely increased his potential to improve. How many outs does he now have? Let's count them, but in doing so we must be careful not to 'double count' certain cards.

For a start, he has nine clubs for the flush. Secondly he has three jacks and three sixes for the straight (note that the J♣ and the 6♣ have already been accounted for with the flush draw – the first example of avoiding double counting). Finally has he two nines and two tens (careful not to include the 10♣). This makes a total of 9 + 3 + 3 + 2 + 2 = 19 outs! Quite an improvement from a mere five.

Tainted Outs

However, it is important to note that Andrew cannot be certain how many of his outs are 'good'. For example if we change the hand slightly so that Barry holds the A♣ instead of the A♠ then we have the following situation.

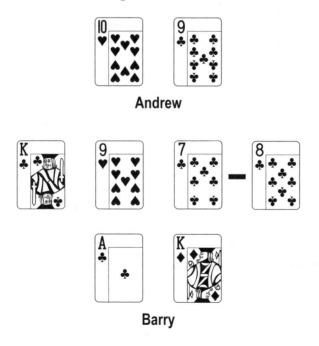

Andrew

Barry

Now Andrew's 'outs' with the clubs are useless. If a random club appears on the river, then he will have a king-high flush but Barry will complete an ace-high flush. In poker parlance, Andrew's club outs are *tainted*. The clubs are no longer good and his 19 outs are reduced to 10. Still, that is a better situation than the five he had on the flop.

In the Real World

Note that – obviously – this is all rather theoretical as neither player actually knows what the other player holds. On the flop Andrew has a pair of nines and – for all he knows – this could currently be the best hand. However, if his opponent bets the hand hard on the flop, then he might assume that he is up against a pair of kings. In that case he has to consider whether he is justified in continuing in the pot, bearing in mind that he currently appears to be behind.

When the turn card comes, he really has no way at all to know whether his opponent has a club (or even two clubs) in his hand, and cannot know precisely how many outs he has – if indeed he has any. For example, if Barry has a hand such as A♣-Q♣, then he has already completed a flush, and Andrew has no outs whatsoever.

 WARNING: Poker is a game if imperfect knowledge. Making judgments about where you stand in the hand and what your chances of improving are is an absolutely key skill in hold'em.

Strong players who – inevitably – have a great deal of experience playing hold'em, recognise the patterns that appear and can make these assessments in an instant. They will know instinctively where they stand in the hand (for good or bad) and have a very good idea how likely they are to take down the pot. This is the skill that you must try to develop to become a consistently winning player.

Playing Hands

In order to keep things simple there will be just two players battling it out. Of course, in actual real-life games (as in the practice hand we played through in Chapter 4) there may well be more players competing for the pot.

Example 1

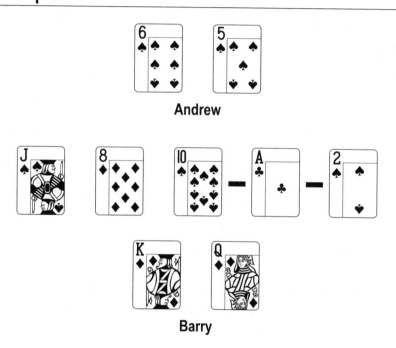

Andrew

Barry

Pre-Flop

Andrew is playing speculatively with suited connectors, whereas Barry has a solid high-card combination which is suited.

Flop

On the flop Andrew had four cards towards a flush with his spade pair matching the two spades on the board. Andrew is thus on a *flush draw* and is hoping for another spade to complete his flush.

Barry could ally the J-10 combination on the board with his K-Q to create K-Q-J-10. This is four cards towards a straight and means that Barry has a straight draw, needing an ace or a nine to complete his straight. Because Barry can complete his straight draw at either end, his hand is an *open-ended straight draw*. A draw to a straight with only one possibility to complete it (e.g. 9-8-7-5 or A-K-Q-T) is known as a *gutshot draw*.

At this point neither side has a made hand, and Barry is currently winning with his king high beating Andrew's jack high. However, both hands have great potential to improve.

Turn

The turn card has done nothing for Andrew's prospects but it has completed Barry's straight (A♣-K♦-Q♦-J♠-10♠). Barry is now well ahead. However, Andrew has *outs* in the form of the missing spade cards. There are no complicating factors and so he has precisely nine outs.

River

It is Andrew's lucky day. He has made his flush on the river. Barry had the best hand but he has been *outdrawn*.

Example 2

Pre-Flop (see next page)

Both players have reasonable high cards. Barry is ahead because although they both have an ace, his jack is better than Andrew's ten. This means that Barry starts as a good favourite in the hand. Andrew will need to improve his holding by hitting a ten on the board (or making an unlikely flush or straight), as pairing his ace will be of no great help (Barry, obviously, will then also have a pair of aces). Barry is also helped by the fact that he has a suited combination.

Flop

On the flop both players have made a pair of aces. The ace is the highest ranking card on the flop, so we can say that both players have *top pair*. At the moment Barry is ahead because he has the better kicker, with his jack outranking Andrew's ten. If nothing much happens to change the structure of the board between now and the river, then Barry will take the pot thanks to his better kicker.

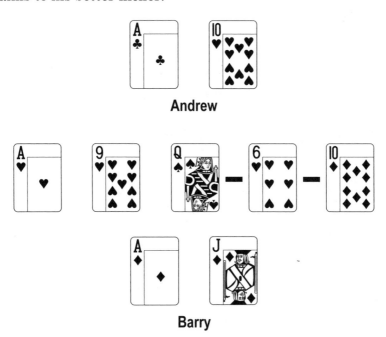

Andrew

Barry

Turn

The turn card helps Andrew slightly. The six is a third heart, and means that Andrew has picked up a flush draw. Barry does not have any hearts in his hand and so the presence of a third heart on board is of no help to him, although – as discussed earlier – Andrew will not know this. The fact that it is a six also does nothing for Barry's hand. However, he is still ahead (better kicker) and Andrew must hit one of his outs on the river to overtake him.

River

Andrew gets lucky again. The 10♦ means that he now has a two-pair hand: aces and tens. Barry has only a pair of aces and so Andrew takes the pot. Barry's better kicker is no longer relevant as Andrew's hand has improved to a better category. Barry had the best hand before the river but he has been *outdrawn* again.

Example 3

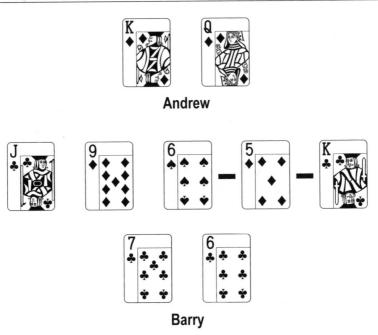

Andrew

Barry

Pre-Flop

Here the players have similar holdings to those from Example 1, but in this case the roles are reversed. Barry is speculating with suited connectors and Andrew has the solid high cards which, in this case, are also suited.

Flop

Here the flop has something for both players. Andrew has not made a pair but the sequence K-Q-J-9 gives him a *gutshot draw* which would be completed with a ten. His king and queen are also higher than any of the board cards and this means that they are *overcards*.

Overcards can be useful because they give you more chances to outdraw a stronger hand. Even if Barry has made top pair with, say J-10, then Andrew can still outdraw him by hitting a king or queen on the turn or river. Consider the situation if Andrew had 7♦-5♦ instead of his holding of K♦-Q♦. Now he still has a gutshot draw (in this case 9-7-6-5, missing the eight) but he no longer has any overcards. If Andrew then makes a pair with either a five or seven coming on board, then it will not help him if Barry happens to hold J-10. Andrew pair of jacks will beat such hands. Andrew's only chance is to complete his gutshot or to receive very helpful cards on the turn and river which result in an improbable flush or three of a kind. Having overcards gives Andrew many extra chances to improve to the winning hand. In this particular situation he has ten outs, these comprising three kings, three queens and four tens (completing the gutshot).

Barry has actually made *bottom pair* with a pair of sixes, but he is probably not thrilled about his hand. He can see that there are two higher cards on the board (J♣-9♦). If Andrew happens to have paired one of those cards, then Barry is struggling and will need to improve. However, as things stand, Barry is actually ahead with his pair of sixes.

Turn

The turn card is a second diamond and this means that Andrew now has a flush draw, although his actual hand is still only king high. The fact that the card is a five means that Barry has picked up a gutshot draw (9-7-6-5). However this is actually irrelevant. Barry is currently winning with his pair of sixes and if an eight does happen to come on the river he will have received a useless piece of luck. His pair is enough to win in any case. It will be particularly irritating for him if the 8♦ appears. He will make a straight but will lose to Andrew's flush.

River

Andrew gets lucky for a third time. For all his wonderful drawing opportunities to flushes and straights, he actually ends up winning with a rather mundane pair of kings. However, this does demonstrate the importance of overcards on the flop.

Example 4

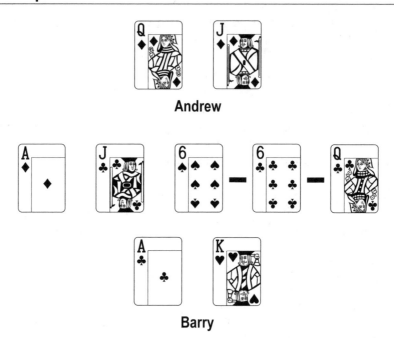

Andrew

Barry

Pre-Flop

Both players have solid high cards. Andrew's are suited and connecting, so he will have more chances to make straights and flushes, whereas Barry has the better high cards so he starts off in the lead.

Flop

Both players make a pair on the flop, but Barry is winning with his pair of aces, against Andrew's pair of jacks. In fact Barry has a strong hand here as he has *top pair, top kicker*, his pair of aces being the best possible pair and his king being the best possible kicker. He is beating any hand that is not stronger than one pair. The flop, being of three different suits, is a *rainbow* flop, making eventual flushes improbable. Notice that there are no real drawing possibilities (to straights or flushes) for either player on the flop.

This situation on the flop is very common with one player having a higher pair than another player. At the moment Andrew has five outs. He needs either a jack or a queen to hit the board in order to improve his hand. The jack will make him a three of a kind, whilst a queen will make him two pairs. In both cases he will overtake Barry's one pair. There are two possible jacks remaining in the deck as well as three queens. So Andrew has five outs.

Turn

The turn card does nothing for either player's hand. In fact, both players have 'improved' from having a one-pair hand to having a two-pair hand. As this 'improvement' is shared, it may appear irrelevant but it has an important effect and actually helps Barry's hand as we will now see.

River

Andrew gets a favourable river card yet again. This time however, it doesn't help him. Although his hand has improved from being two pair, jacks and sixes, to two pair, queens and jacks, the problem is that Andrew has a bigger two pair – aces and sixes. Now we can see how the turn card subtly helped Barry's hand. It reduced Andrew's outs from five to two – only a jack on the river could help him.

Example 5

Pre-Flop (see next page)

Here we have a classic pre-flop confrontation with a medium strength pair up against two unpaired high cards. The most likely way that Barry can overtake Andrew is by pairing one of his cards. However, with five cards to come on the board his chances of pairing before the river are approximately 50%.

Flop

This is a fantastic flop for Andrew. He has a pair of nines in his hand and the third nine on the flop gives him three of a kind.

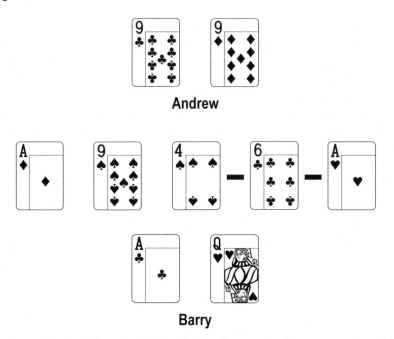

Andrew

Barry

Barry will also like the look of this flop as he has top pair with a very good kicker. He is not to know that Andrew has flopped a monster hand and that he is in big trouble.

A set is nearly always a very powerful holding. In the above example, the only way that Barry could possibly have a better hand is by having a pair of aces in his hand when he would have flopped a set of aces. We have seen in previous examples how a hand such as one pair can often be overtaken – it is much, much harder to overtake a set. Andrew's main worry here is that Barry might have two spades in his hand, giving him a chance to make a flush. This would be Barry's only real-istic chance to overtake Andrew but, as we know, he doesn't have such a hand. In fact, although Barry has a good hand – and one that he will probably play strongly, he already has al-most no chance to win.

Turn

The turn card does nothing for either player's hand, but An-drew will be pleased that a further spade did not arrive. There is now no card in the deck that can give Barry a winning hand. In poker parlance, he is *drawing dead*.

River

The ace on the river gives Barry trip aces, meaning that he now has three of a kind. His three aces rank higher than Andrew's three nines – does that mean he has overtaken him? No! The pair on board means that Andrew's hand is now 9-9-9-A-A. Andrew has a full house: nines full of aces. Barry's improvement has been in vain. This demonstrates just what a powerful hand a set is. Barry improved hugely on the river and yet could still not overtake his opponent.

Example 6

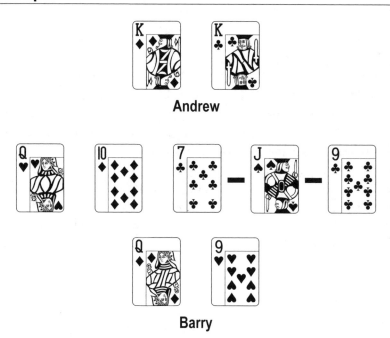

Andrew

Barry

Pre-Flop

Andrew starts off this deal with a very strong hand – a pair of kings. Barry has a reasonable holding with two high cards, but he will need to be very lucky to overtake Andrew in this hand.

He will probably need to make trips, a two-pair hand with both a queen and a nine coming on the board, or he will need to make a straight.

Flop

The flop offers a little help to Barry as he has made a pair. However, Andrew has an *overpair* – his kings being higher than any of the cards on the board – and knows that he is in a strong position. However, note that although Andrew's hand is good, it is not nearly as good as the set he was holding in the previous example. On that occasion, Barry needed to have one precise hand – a pair of aces – to be beating him. Here there are many more hands that actually beat Andrew's:

> A-A: this gives Barry a better overpair.
>
> Q-Q, 10-10 or 7-7: these hands would give Barry the dreaded set.
>
> Q-10, Q-7, 10-7: these hands give Barry a two-pair hand.

At the moment, however, Barry needs either a queen or a nine to overtake Andrew. He thus has five outs.

Remember also that on the previous hand it was almost impossible for the set to be overtaken. Here Barry already has five outs to make the winning hand, and he has two opportunities (the turn and river) to get lucky. Andrew is a good favourite but Barry certainly has chances.

Turn

The turn card is a useful one for Barry as – although he is still behind – he now has an open-ended straight draw (Q-J-10-9) which generates extra outs for him.

River

The river is a card which helps Barry. He has now improved to a two-pair hand (queens and nines). This looks like good news for him. Is he now winning? No! The nine has placed the sequence Q-J-10-9 on board and Andrew has the vital king to complete the straight. His straight beats Barry's two pair and he takes the pot. The 9♣ was a *tainted out* for Barry

The turn card (J♠) has turned out to be Barry's nemesis. Had a random low card appeared on the turn, followed by the nine on the river, then his two pair would have triumphed.

Focusing on Outs

We will now examine the concept of outs more carefully. All of the following situations occur after the flop and turn cards have been dealt and we will consider who is currently winning and how many outs the weaker hand has. At all times we must look carefully for the possibility of *tainted outs*.

Example 1

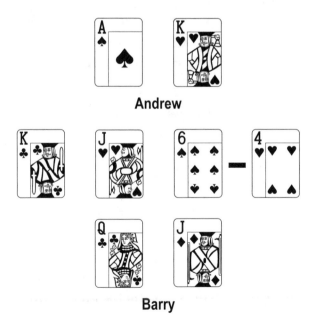

Andrew

Barry

Andrew is winning with a pair of kings against a pair of jacks. Barry has five outs: two jacks and three queens. This is the standard situation where you have a battle between pairs of different rank – the weaker side will usually be playing for five outs.

Example 2

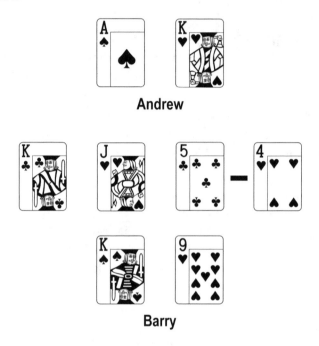

Andrew

Barry

Andrew is winning. Both players have a pair of kings, but Andrew has the crucial ace kicker. Barry has just three outs – the three missing nines. These will give him a two-pair hand. Note that this situation is considerably worse for the weaker hand than the one in Example 1 – the problem being the shared king. Strangely – Barry's chances would actually be improved if he held a weaker hand! With a hand such as J-10 or 6-5 he would actually have five outs rather than just three.

Example 3

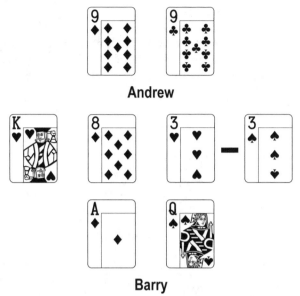

Andrew is winning with a pair of nines. Barry has six outs: three aces and three queens will give him a higher pair.

Example 4

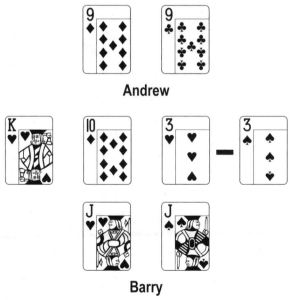

Barry is winning with a pair of jacks against a pair of nines. Andrew has just two outs – the two missing nines.

 WARNING: Pairs, especially big pairs, are often good hands to play. However, if you are losing to a higher pair then you are in bad shape, as it is very difficult to improve to a stronger hand.

Example 5

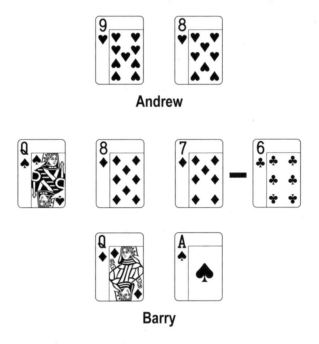

Andrew

Barry

Barry is winning with a pair of queens against a pair of eights. Andrew has 13 outs: four tens and four fives complete a straight, while three nines and two eights improve him to three of a kind and two pairs respectively.

NOTE: When the board becomes coordinated with straightening and flushing cards, then it becomes likely that weaker hands will have a lot more outs.

Example 6

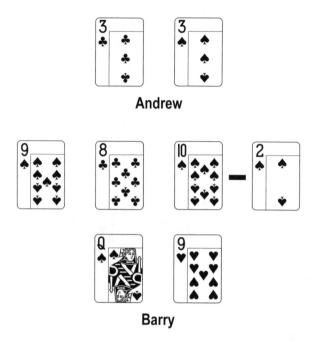

Andrew

Barry

Barry's pair of nines is beating Andrew's pair of threes. Andrew has just two outs – the missing threes. A spade will give him a flush, but that would not help as Barry's Q♠ will give him a higher flush. Note that Barry has an irrelevant draw to a straight with any jack giving him Q-J-10-9-8. He is winning anyway, so he doesn't need to improve.

 WARNING: Low pairs that receive no immediate help on the flop are very poor holdings as they are often playing with just two outs.

Example 7

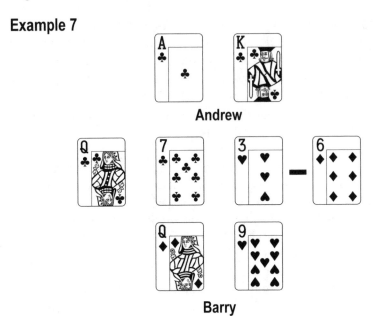

Andrew is behind but has 15 outs: nine clubs to complete the flush, as well as three aces and three kings to make a bigger pair.

Example 8

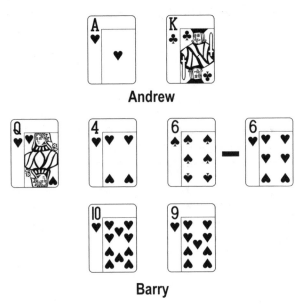

Barry is winning with a flush against Andrew's pair of kings. Andrew has seven outs: his A♥ means that any of the remaining hearts will put four hearts on the board and enable him to make a bigger flush on the river.

Example 9

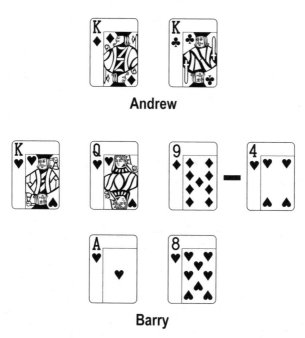

Andrew

Barry

Barry is winning with a flush against Andrew's three of a kind kings. Andrew has ten outs: he can complete a full house with any of three queens, three nines or three fours, while the missing king (in poker parlance, the *case* king) will give him four of a kind.

Example 10

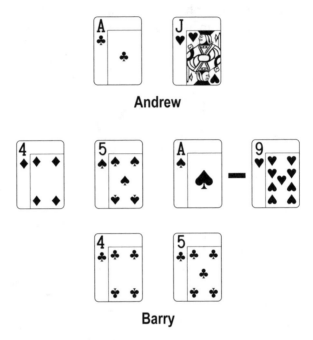

Andrew

Barry

Barry is winning with two pairs, fives and fours, against Andrew's single pair of aces. Andrew has eight outs: two aces and three jacks are 'normal' ways to win, but he can also win if any of the three missing nines arrives, since this will improve him to two pairs, aces and nines. In that case one of Barry's pair of fours will be *counterfeited* by the higher pair on the board.

Exercise Six

In each of the following situations, work out who has the best hand and consider carefully how many outs the weaker hand has. Be warned, some of them are quite tricky.

(Answers on page 255.)

Question 1)

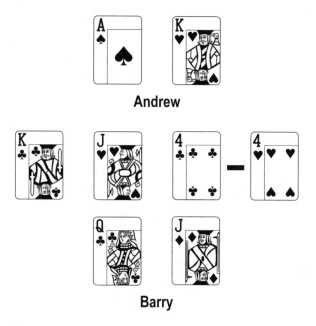

Andrew

Barry

Question 2)

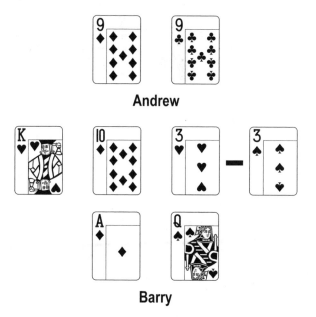

Andrew

Barry

Question 3)

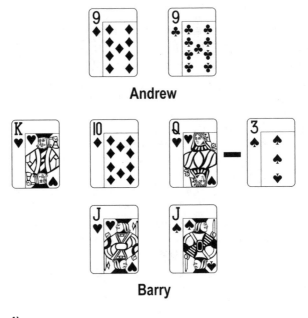

Andrew

Barry

Question 4)

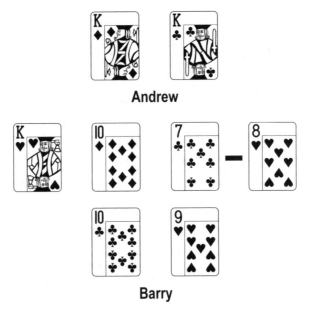

Andrew

Barry

Question 5)

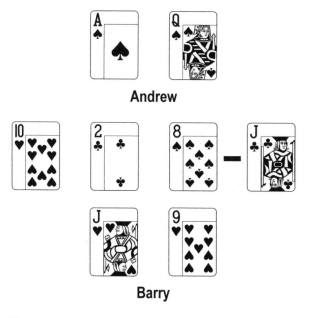

Andrew

Barry

Question 6)

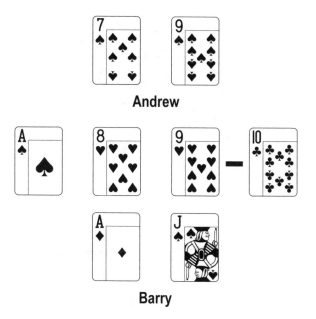

Andrew

Barry

Question 7)

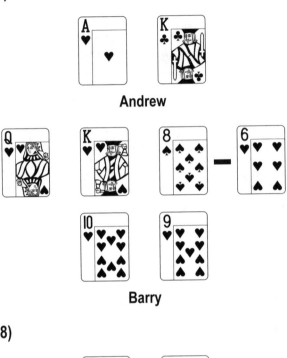

Andrew

Barry

Question 8)

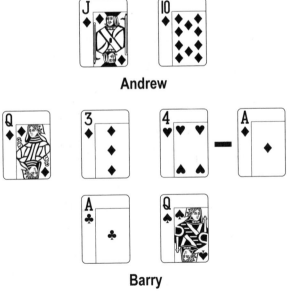

Andrew

Barry

Question 9)

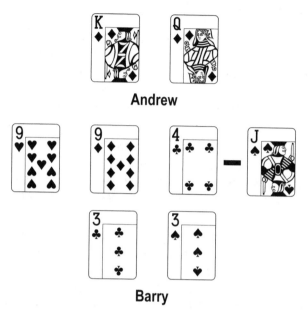

Andrew

Barry

Question 10)

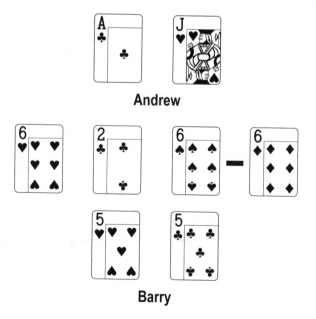

Andrew

Barry

Developing a Feel

Now that we have played through a number of deals you should have some feel for how a hand can develop. However, you will need to refine this further. Rather than filling up the book with hundreds of further examples, I suggest that you get a deck of cards and spend a couple of hours just dealing out hands.

Pretend that you are playing heads-up and expose both your hand and that of your 'opponent'. Of course, hold'em isn't played like this, but the exercise will be a good one for you to further refine your feel for how hands develop and improve – or don't as the case may be.

You can start by just dealing out all the cards randomly. However, as discussed earlier, you will only actually play around 20-25% of the hands that you are dealt, and so if you just give yourself and your opponent random cards you will witness a number of rather pointless battles between hands such as 9♣-2♥ and 6♦-J♠.

I would therefore suggest that after a while you deal out more natural starting hands and play out a number of deals with these starting hands fixed. This will also give you a good feel for how certain hands tend to get on against certain other hands. I would suggest the following battles:

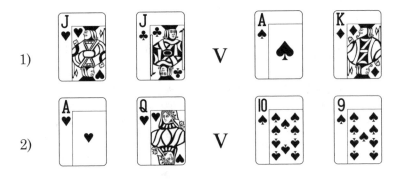

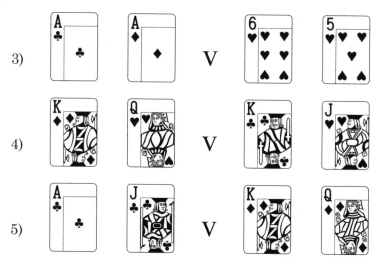

3) A♣ A♦ V 6♥ 5♥

4) K♦ Q♥ V K♣ J♥

5) A♣ J♣ V K♦ Q♦

In each case give the first hand to yourself, the latter hand to your 'opponent' and then play out the deal in the standard way: three flop cards, then the turn and finally the river. Repeat this about 20 times for each pairing. Note that in each case you have the better starting hand. View the play with the following thoughts:

1) What sort of flops are good for me?

2) If I get a good flop, how often am I getting outdrawn by the river?

3) If the flop is bad and I get outdrawn, how often can I turn it around by the river?

Chapter Six

Hold'em Play:
Basic Principles

- ♣ Odds and Pot Odds
- ♣ Implied Odds
- ♣ Exercise Seven
- ♣ Position

Before discussing how to play specific hands in the pre-flop stage, I would like to introduce various concepts that will be crucial to the understanding of what you are trying to achieve when playing hold'em.

Odds and Pot Odds

I have occasionally mentioned probabilities in the earlier text. However, now that we are about to get into the nitty-gritty of hold'em play we need to formalise exactly what is meant by odds, and also to introduce the concept of pot odds.

Odds

The odds of a particular event are a representation of the chances of it happening and are expressed as x-to-y where, more often than not, y is 1. 'y' is the chance that the event will happen and 'x' is the chance that it won't. Thus if you roll a normal dice the chance that a six will appear is 5-to-1, i.e. there is one chance that it will happen and five chances that it won't. If you shuffle a pack of cards, cut them and then look at the top card, the chance that it will be an ace is 12-to-1.

Odds are crucial in all forms of poker, and poker texts constantly discuss odds in numerous different situations. For example if you have two clubs and the flop comes with precisely two clubs, then you have a flush draw. What are the odds of this flush being completed on the turn?

There are 52 cards in the deck and you can see five of them. There are thus 47 unseen cards. Nine of these (the missing clubs) are helpful and will complete your draw. Thirty-eight are unhelpful and will not. Thus your chances of completing your flush draw on the turn are 38-to-9. This expression is rather unwieldy but it is fairly close to 4-to-1. Thus your chances are about 1 in 5 or about 20%. An approximation such as this will be fine for real-life decisions.

Pot Odds

The discussion of odds leads naturally on to considerations of pot odds. Pot odds basically represent the amount of money you have to put into the pot to call a bet relative to the amount of money currently in the pot. Thus if there is $30 in the pot and you need to call a bet of $10 you are receiving pot odds of 3-to-1. If there is $100 in the pot and you have to call a bet of $20 your pot odds are 5-to-1.

There are many decisions in hold'em which are purely dependent upon the pot odds that you are receiving. Here is a simple example:

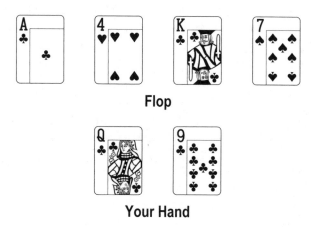

Flop

Your Hand

Here you have a flush draw and there is one card remaining to be dealt. There is $80 in the pot, you have just one opponent and they bet $10. You are 'certain' that they hold either an ace or a king in their hand, so your only chance to win the pot is by completing your flush – making a pair of queens or nines will be no good. Should you call?

To work out the answer we need to calculate the odds of completing our draw and then consider the pot odds. We do not have to do this to six decimal places – a rough estimate will be fine. From our previous calculations we know that the odds of completing a flush draw with just one card are approximately

4-to-1. Here we are being offered pot odds of 8-to-1. The pot odds are very much better than our actual odds and we should call.

If the pot were instead much smaller at just $30 and the bet remained at $10 then our pot odds are just 3-to-1. This is worse than the 4-to-1 chance of completing our flush and we should fold.

If you are not convinced of this look what happens if we play each scenario out five times.

Firstly the pot is $80 and we call for $10. With average luck we will make our flush one time in five. Thus on four occasions we will simply lose the $10 we have invested while on the other occasion we will hit and end up winning $80. Thus our bet (actually call, to be precise) shows a profit of $40 in five outings or an average of $8 per play.

We can make a similar calculation when the pot is $30 and now we see that – over five attempts – we will still lose $40. However, our win will only be worth $30 and so we will end up $10 down over five plays. Thus now our call has a negative expectation of $2 per play and we are better off folding.

Note that folding in the first example would be a big mistake, whereas calling in the second example is a much smaller mistake.

Typical Drawing Hands

Here are some typical drawing situations and their odds. Hopefully by now you will be able to recognise these drawing situations and have a good feel for the number of outs each hand holds.

Obviously you can never precisely know your opponent's hand, but situations frequently arise in which it is pretty clear how many cards are likely to win the pot for you.

Flush Draw with Overcards

Example:

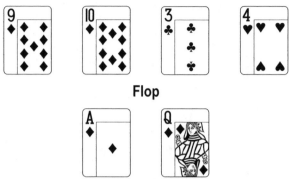

Flop

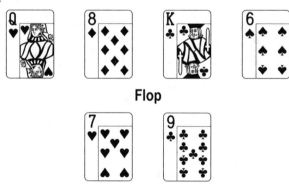

Your Hand

Your opponent holds: a pair and kicker below queens, e.g. J-10

Number of outs: 15

Exact chance to hit: 31-to-15

Rough approximation: 2-to-1

Open-ended Straight Draw

Example:

Flop

Your Hand

Your opponent holds: a high pair, e.g. A-K

Number of outs: 8

Exact chance to hit: 38-to-8

Rough approximation: 5-to-1

Two Overcards

Example:

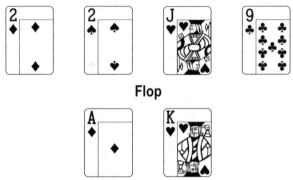

Flop

Your Hand

Your opponent holds: a pair lower than kings, e.g. J-10

Number of outs: 6

Exact chance to hit: 40-to-6

Rough approximation: 7-to-1

Gutshot Draw

Example:

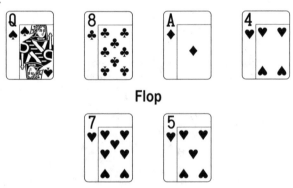

Flop

Your Hand

Your opponent holds: any remotely decent pair!

Number of outs: 4

Exact chance to hit: 42-to-4

Rough approximation: 10-to-1

Implied Odds

When we consider pot odds we are looking at a specific situation – it costs a certain amount to call a bet and there is a certain amount of money in the pot. This generates a specific 'value' for our bet. However, there are occasions when you will want to call a bet even though you are sure that you are currently losing and the current pot odds do not justify a call. Such situations rely on implied odds.

Consider the following:

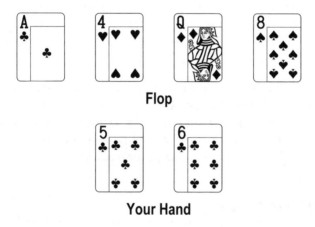

Flop

Your Hand

Let's assume there is $90 in the pot and it is $10 to call your opponent's bet. Your opponent has bet the hand strongly and you know that he has a decent hand – probably a high pair. Your only chance is to complete your gutshot with a seven. Should you call the bet?

Working strictly on pot odds we calculate as follows. It is most unlikely that our opponent has a seven (he almost certainly has two high cards) so there are four winning cards for us out of 44 unseen cards. This generates odds of 40-to-4 or 10-to-1. The pot is offering us odds of 9-to-1. Therefore we should fold.

However, if we call the bet and the miracle seven does indeed appear on the river, consider what will happen. Our opponent will not be worried, as it will be hard for him to believe that this innocent-looking seven could possibly have helped us. He will therefore bet. We have the nut hand and raise. He will probably call this bet and will thus end up losing a total of $20 on the river. So, in addition to the $90 that was in the pot on the turn we have accumulated an extra $20 when we hit our seven (if we don't hit the seven it doesn't matter – we will fold on the river and will not lose any more money). This makes a total of $110. So, you could argue that the true pot odds for the call on the turn were 11-to-1 and not 9-to-1. As we already know, the chance of completing our hand is 10-to-1 and so now the call has a positive rather than a negative value. This is what *implied odds* are all about – the implication that you can make more money than is currently in the pot when you do hit your hand. Implied odds are also an important concept in pre-flop play – as we shall soon see.

 TIP: Do not get carried away trying to calculate with precise accuracy the benefits of any play involving pot odds and/or implied odds. Many of them are borderline. The important thing is to understand the principle so that you avoid wildly incorrect decisions.

Exercise Seven

(Answers on page 257.)

1) You shuffle a pack of cards, cut them and then look at the top card. What are the chances that it is a heart?

2) You shuffle a pack of cards, cut them and then look at the top card. What are the chances that it is a black ace?

3) You hold A-K, you opponent holds 10-8 and the board is J-10-6-6. What are your chances of improving to the winning hand on the river?

4) You hold 9-7 and you are certain that your opponent has a big overpair, either aces or kings. The board is 9-6-5-2. What are your chances of improving to the winning hand on the river?

5) You hold 9♣-8♣ and the board is A♠-9♥-4♣-3♦. Your opponent has bet strongly throughout the hand and you are sure he has an ace with a good kicker. There is $40 in the pot and it is $4 to call. Do you have pot odds to call?

6) You hold 9♣-8♣ and the board is A♠-9♥-4♣-4♦. Your opponent has bet strongly throughout the hand and you are sure he has an ace with a good kicker. There is $40 in the pot and it is $4 to call. Do you have pot odds to call?

Position

Position is an absolutely fundamental concept in hold'em. The key point with hold'em is that your position (with regards to when the betting comes to you) is fixed throughout the entire deal. If you have bad position (i.e. the betting comes to you early in the action) then you are stuck with it for the whole hand. If you are in the favourable situation of having late position, then this is an advantage you carry with you for the whole hand. In this respect the game differs from stud where the player who is obliged to open the betting can change from round to round.

The only slight exception to the fact that position is absolutely fixed in hold'em is with regard to the blinds. On the pre-flop round of betting the blinds are in the advantageous position of being last to speak. However, on all post-flop rounds the blinds will speak first.

It is a great advantage to have good position and it can result in saving bets that would otherwise have been lost, and gaining bets which might have slipped through your fingers if you had bad position. Let's see how this works in practice.

What happens with Bad Position

Imagine that after the pre-flop play there are four players left in the pot including you. You are first to speak. The flop comes down and you like the look of it – so you bet. The second player now raises, the third player calls and the fourth player now re-raises. With all this heavy action your holding suddenly appears a lot less attractive and – rather than call two more bets (the raise and the re-raise) you decide to fold. However, this cost you a bet because you opened the betting.

Next time you are in this position you decide to play more circumspectly and you check. Your plan is that if the action heats up before it gets round to you, you will fold. However, it turns out that nobody has very much and the round gets checked out. Now the turn card is dealt and it is a bad one for you. It does nothing for your hand but has helped one of your opponents to overtake you. Bad news. However, if you had bet the flop in the first place this player would have had to fold and you would have gone on to win the pot. However, you are not psychic and you didn't know that.

What happens with Good Position

Now look what happens if you are in late position and the same two scenarios occur. In the first example, the opposition have some good hands; someone bets early on and there is a caller and then before the action gets to you there is a raise. Now you get the message, you discard your hand and you didn't waste a bet.

The second example also works in your favour. You have your moderate hand and are not entirely sure if you want to bet it or not. However, before you make your decision you see all three of your three opponents checking. It is therefore likely that no-one has very much, and so you decide your moderate hand is worth a bet. It turns out that they do indeed not have very much, they all fold and you take the pot. The player who got lucky first time round never gets a chance this time. He was obliged to reveal that his hand was weak (he checked) and you bet him out of the pot.

 TIP: In poker, as with many things in life, information is power. When you have good position you gain information, when you have bad position you don't.

Chapter Seven

Pre-Flop Play: General Principles

- ♣ Position and Pre-Flop Play
- ♣ Domination
- ♣ Small Cards
- ♣ Pairs and Non-Pairs
- ♣ Suited or Offsuit
- ♣ Entering the Pot
- ♣ Playing from the Blinds

Position and Pre-Flop Play

In the previous chapter we looked at the idea of position, and saw how it can be a very important factor for the play of hands. Position is also critical in pre-flop play, and having bad position is again a serious drawback. The fact that you have to make decisions about betting before knowing anything else about any of the other hands at the table means that you need a very strong hand to get involved. As your position improves around the table, this requirement becomes less stringent and you can then play more hands.

The concept of position is something that many beginning players find hard to understand. They will happily join in the game with all kinds of feeble holdings in early position, as they realise that given a helpful enough flop then 'any two cards can win'.

 WARNING: Playing bad hands out of position is probably the single worst error that is made by weak hold'em players.

In order to understand why it is just so bad to play weak hands in early position, consider the following.

The Game of 100

Let us invent a new game which bears a passing similarity to hold'em. As with hold'em, there are ten players around the table, but instead of a pack of playing cards we are using a 'pack' of 100 cards with the numbers 1 to 100 on them. The pack is shuffled and each player is dealt one card. As with hold'em there will be a round of betting, during which players may fold, call, or even raise. There will only be one round of betting. When the betting is complete, there will be a showdown and the player with the highest card will win.

Let us imagine that you are now first to speak. How good would your card have to be before you decide to bet?

You know that you have to beat nine other random cards, so you need something pretty good – what do you think that would be? 85? 90? Perhaps even 92 or 93?

There is no doubt a mathematical formula which can give you the exact point at which you should bet rather than fold, but I think that most players would intuitively feel that they needed to hold at least number 90 to risk a bet.

Now let us imagine that five players have already folded so there are only four other random hands for you to beat. Now how high a card would you need? 80? Maybe just a little more – perhaps 83? Again I am sure that a mathematical formula could generate the 'correct' figure, but it should be obvious that this number will be a fair bit less than the number needed if you had to open the betting from early position.

Now let us assume that seven players have folded and you have just two opponents. Now you might take a chance with something quite a bit lower, maybe just 70, or even 65. You will also notice that now another possibility arises. With quite a poor number, say just 35, you might consider betting anyway on the grounds that your two opponents might not have very high numbers and might just fold. Thus you might bet with 35 and the next player, holding a 45, might fold and you could get to take the pot with your 'bluff'. Such a strategy was less attractive when you had more opponents as then there was obviously a greater chance that you would run into a powerhouse with someone holding a really big number such as 98, 99 or even 100. As the number of opponents decreases, so does the possibility that there is a big card out against you.

Obviously this 'game' is a very crude approximation to hold'em. In hold'em there will be post-flop play and any holding can then beat any other holding with a favourable flop. However, the important principle is that when you get involved in a pot you should do so in circumstances that give you a good chance to be (initially at least) holding the best hand. If you are constantly entering pots with insufficiently strong hands relative to your position, you will find yourself involved in endless uphill struggles.

Without wishing to sound overly dramatic, when you enter a pot, you make a decision that you are going to war. If you are going to war you want to make sure that there is an excellent chance that your weapons are stronger than those of your opponents. If you commence hostilities armed with a pea-shooter and your opponent unleashes a bazooka, you are going to get blown away more often than not.

Domination

Another key concept in hold'em pre-flop play is that of domination. Some hands *dominate* other hands which makes it hard for the weaker hand to overtake the stronger one. Let's consider some examples.

1) Your Opponent holds 9-9 and You hold Q-J

Your opponent currently has a stronger hand than you, but your hand is not dominated. Any jack or queen will give you a pair higher than you opponent's nines and will improve you to the winning hand. Your opponent is a slight favourite; if the hand is played out to the river the chances are approximately 55%-45% in favour of your opponent.

2) Your Opponent holds A-J and You hold K-Q

As before, you are behind, but your hand is not dominated. Kings and queens are outs for you – both your cards are 'live'. If the hand is played out to the river the chances are approximately 60%-40% in your opponent's favour.

3) Your Opponent holds 9-9 and You hold A-6

Now you are partially dominated. An ace will help you but a six won't. This is a poor situation. In hold'em you want both of your cards to be working for you and here the six is a bit of a passenger and you are really just playing with an ace. Your opponent is a good favourite; if the hand is played out to the river the chances are approximately 70%-30% in favour of your opponent.

4) Your Opponent Holds 9-9 and You Hold 7-6

Now your hand is badly dominated. Hitting either a six or a seven on its own is not going to help you as it merely gives you a pair weaker than your opponent's nines. You will need to see a substantial improvement on the board in order to overtake your opponent. You will need something like 7-6, 6-6, 7-7 or an unlikely straight to materialise – and all of these are longshots. Your opponent is a big favourite; if the hand is played out to the river the chances are approximately 85%-15% in your opponent's favour.

There are two other common situations where domination occurs:

1) A Higher Pair Versus a Lower Pair, e.g. K-K v J-J

Now the weaker hand probably needs to hit one of only two missing jacks to improve to the best hand. The jacks are badly dominated. If the hand is played to the river the higher pair triumphs by approximately 82%-18%.

2) A Shared Card, e.g. A-Q v Q-10

Here the weaker hand is reduced to trying to hit a ten, as pairing the queen will also make a pair for the stronger side who will then have the better kicker. This is again a very good situation for the stronger hand which will come out on top by a ratio of approximately 72%-28%.

We saw many of these situations occurring when we played through hands and watched how they develop in Chapter 5.

Small Cards

In general you want to play big cards in hold'em. This should be obvious – big cards can make big hands: big pairs, big two pairs, big sets, top straights, big full houses etc. Small cards make small hands, are easily dominated and tend to lose to big hands. Thus, there is a very simple rule about small cards:

 WARNING: Very simple rule to remember about small cards: do not play them!

In lower limit hold'em games many players flout this rule and will happily enter the pot with 7♣-6♣, 4♥-3♥, 9♦-8♥, J♠-8♠. Occasionally they will get lucky and make a straight or a flush and win a decent-sized pot. In the short term this will be a good result, but in the long term it is a disaster as it will merely encourage them to play such cards again.

There are so many problems with playing small cards that it is hard to know where to start, but let's try anyway. A holding like 8♣-7♣ can be playable in certain circumstances, but if you are consistently playing it against stronger hands you will run into all sorts of trouble.

Typical Small Card Problems

Let's consider the problems that arise when you are playing a hand like 8♣-7♣ that do not arise when you have a solid hand such as K♣-Q♣:

1) You hit a Pair on the Flop

When you make a pair on the flop, it is always good if you have top pair, i.e. if there are three cards of different rank, then your pair is formed by matching the top card. If you do not have top pair, you will always face tricky decisions as you can never be sure whether someone else has made a higher pair. With K♣-Q♣ it is quite likely that you will have top pair as the only possible overcard is an ace. Thus your only difficult hands will be ones with quite specific flops such as A-Q-7 or A-K-2. Of course, you can make top pair and have a very good kicker and still be losing, but at least you will not have difficult decisions to make during the play. You will bet the hand hard and it will just be bad luck when you lose.

However, when you make a pair with 8♣-7♣, there will nearly always be an overcard (or overcards) and it will be much harder to know where you stand. Consider flops such as K-8-3, Q-7-4 or J-10-8. In all cases you have a pair, but the flops are dangerous for you because there are overcards to your pair on the board which may well have enabled players to make bigger pairs than you.

Consider the final case – J-10-8.

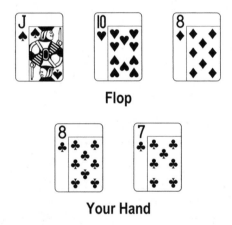

Flop

Your Hand

Although there are two overcards to your pair, you might think this looks quite good because you also have a chance to make a straight if a nine arrives. However, note that a nine will generate the sequence J-10-9-8. This will indeed give you a straight, but it will be beaten by anyone who has a queen in their hand as they will now have a higher straight (their Q-J-10-9-8 will beat your J-10-9-8-7).

There is a further point here. Another of your improving cards is a seven which will give you two pair. However, if a seven comes on the board then the sequence J-10-8-7 has materialised and an opponent only needs a nine to complete a straight.

This is typical of what can happen when you play small cards.

You are constantly running the danger of making second-best hands where you will feel obliged to pay off the stronger hand.

2) You flop a Really Good Hand

Even when you hit wonderful flops you will still face problems when you play low cards. Here is an example:

1) You have 8♣-7♣ and the flop is J♠-10♥-9♥.

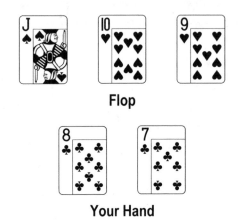

Flop

Your Hand

Wonderful! You have flopped a straight. Surely this is fantastic and justifies your speculative play with the low cards? No – it doesn't. You can lose from this position surprisingly easily. If a seven comes, anyone with an eight will tie; if an eight comes, anyone with a queen will beat you and anyone with a seven will tie; if a queen comes, anyone with a king will beat you and anyone with an eight will tie; if a king comes, anyone with a queen will beat you. If you have many opponents, you will be quite fortunate if your hand is still good at the river. Consider this: with just one opponent, holding Q♥-J♦ you are 'only' a 2-to-1 favourite to win by the river.

Let's assume that instead you had played stronger cards and started with K♣-Q♣. Now you have still flopped a straight but you have a rock solid hand. Critically, you have the *higher* end of the straight. You will be unlucky if queens and/or kings arrive, but even then you will still probably split the pot. Suddenly an eight becomes a great card for you.

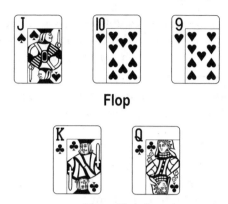

Flop

Your Hand

Anyone with a seven might stick around with their low straight, whereas a player with a queen will have a straight, but you will have a stronger one (theirs goes up to the queen but yours goes up to the king). You can make a lot of money with your hand.

However, despite all of this, low cards are occasionally playable, but it has to be in exactly the right circumstances. As a beginning player you *could* adopt the following very crude rule about pre-flop play – you will only consider playing your hand if:

1) You have a pocket pair *or*

2) If both of you cards are ten or higher.

Everything else you will fold.

I am not going to recommend that you play like this but, even if you did, you would be making very few mistakes.

Pairs and Non-Pairs

Before we move on to a discussion of how to play specific hands pre-flop, we need to discuss the difference between playing with a pair pre-flop (of whatever rank) and playing non-paired cards. When you play a pair your hand is pretty much defined pre-flop. Pairs are hands that more often than not fail to improve on the flop and even by the river. Of course, if you have a big pair that may not matter – a big pair is often enough to win a pot even if it remains unimproved all the way to the river.

If you are playing a pair you – obviously – would like your pair to be as high as possible. The higher your pair the less likely it is that overcards to your pair will appear on the board, and the more chance there is that your pair will stand on its own two feet. If you are lucky enough to be dealt a pair of kings, then the only cards which can arrive on the flop which are immediately dangerous for you are aces. However, if you have a pair of tens, then you will have to be concerned any time a jack, queen, king or ace appears on the flop. If you are playing a pair of fives, then it is highly improbable that a flop will appear which features only cards ranking lower. Of course, an overcard appearing to your pair is not necessarily the end of the world, but it will serve to make you more cautious in the way you handle your pair.

The following table demonstrates how quickly the chance of an overcard arriving on the flop increases as the ranking of your pair decreases.

Holding	Chance of No Overcards on the Flop
K-K	77.5%
Q-Q	58.6%
J-J	43%
10-10	30.5%
9-9	20.7%
8-8	13.3%
7-7	7.9%
6-6	4.2%

The problem with playing a pair on the flop when there are overcards is that, if someone does have a better hand than you then your chances of improvement are minimal. Non-paired hands have a much better chance to overtake stronger hands.

Consider the following scenarios. In each case the flop will be Q♣-10♠-4♥ and another player holds a queen to make top pair.

1) You, the hero, hold J♥-J♣ and the flop is Q♣-10♠-4♥. Your opponent, the villain, holds A♠-Q♦.

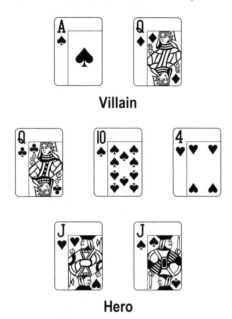

Villain

Hero

Here there are only two cards (the missing jacks) that will improve your hand. The chances of one of these arriving on the turn is a mere 23½-to-1. Not good. If this hand is played to the river, your chances of winning are just 12.5%. Also not good.

2) You hold J♥-10♥ and the flop is again Q♣-10♠-4♥.

Once more you suspect that the villain has a queen. Here your hand is actually – in principle – weaker than in the previous example. You have only a pair of tens instead of a pair of jacks. Now, however, there are five cards that will immediately improve your hand – three jacks and two tens.

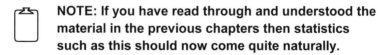

NOTE: If you have read through and understood the material in the previous chapters then statistics such as this should now come quite naturally.

The chance of an immediate improvement to your hand on the turn is now 9-to-1. Not great, but a big improvement over the 23½-to-1 when you had the pair of jacks.

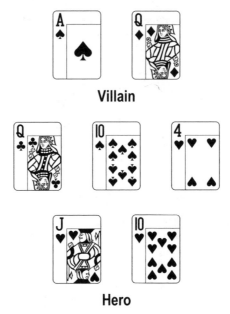

Villain

Hero

Furthermore you now have more possibilities to receive helpful cards on the turn. For example Q♣-10♠-4♥-3♥:

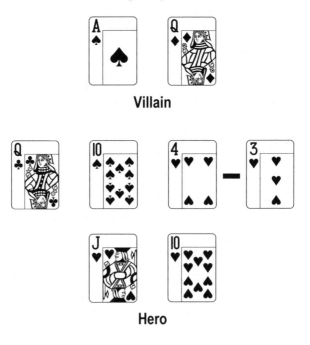

Villain

Hero

Now suddenly you have a flush draw which generates an extra nine outs for you on the river.

If the flop situation is played out to the river then your chances of winning are approximately 26%. After receiving the helpful 3♥ on the turn your chances of improving to the winning hand are 32%.

3) You hold K♥-J♥ and the flop is again Q♣-10♠-4♥.

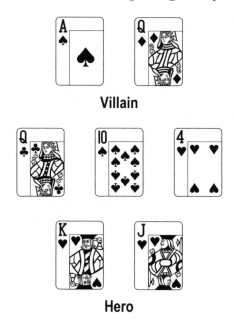

Villain

Hero

Now you have the weakest actual hand of all, with just king high. However, your K-J has interwoven nicely with the Q-T on board to give you an open-ended straight draw.

Now – quick – how many outs do you have against your opponent's A-Q?

The answer is 10. You have four nines and three aces for a straight and three kings to overtake the villain's pair of queens with a pair of kings. Of course, you cannot know that the villain has an ace in his hand, depriving you of one out, but you would suspect that less than 100% of your outs were good. For example if he held K-Q, then your outs to the kings would be no good (I hope you can see why) and you would have a total of eight outs with the straight draw. The chance of an immediate improvement to your hand on the turn with an open-ended straight draw is a much more healthy 4-to-1.

If the flop situation is played out to the river then you have a 40% chance of winning with your open-ended straight draw and overcard.

A good player will know – at a glance – that there are approximately 10 outs for the hero in this situation. He cannot know precisely how many there are, but he will know that it in principle (if none of the outs were tainted) it is 11, but likely to be fractionally lower. He will know that it is not as low as five nor is it as high as 15. This will enable him to make good decisions as to how to play the hand.

 NOTE: To become a strong hold'em player you need to be able to understand situations like this instinctively.

That's why we have put so much emphasis on them in the earlier chapters.

In Summary

The board: Q♣-10♠-4♥, Villain's hand: A♠-Q♦

Hero's hand	Chance of winning by river
J♥-J♠	12.5%
J♥-T♥	26%
K♥-J♥	40%

Notice the curious feature in that the weaker the hero's current hand, the more likely he is to actually win the pot. When you are behind in a pot you are much better off with drawing possibilities than with a made hand.

Suited or Offsuit

Approximately one time in four you will be dealt a hand in which your cards are of the same suit. Many weak players fall in love with these hands and find all sorts of excuses to play feeble hands just because they are suited. Occasionally they make a flush and win a decent-sized pot, but this only helps to reinforce their love affair with suited cards. Much more often they simply dribble away unnecessary bets chasing hopeless longshots. The occasional decent pot which they win in no way compensates for the horrible leakage of bets that they suffer when their flush fails to materialise.

 NOTE: A 'leak' is a negative characteristic of a player's style which – in the long run – will cost them money.

How Likely is a Flush?

So, if you start with a couple of suited cards how likely are you to end up with a flush? The sad fact is – not very. However, do not despair. The laws of mathematics do not apply solely to you – they apply to your opponents as well. Many of your opponents will be playing far too many suited combinations. They will make very few flushes and you will benefit from the unnecessary bets that they contribute to the pot.

To see how likely a flush is to come in we need to do a little maths. There are three ways you can make a flush if you play suited cards. Let's assume you have two hearts.

1) The flop can come with three hearts and you have a flush at once.

2) The flop can come with two hearts, giving you a flush draw. You then complete your flush by the river.

3) The flop can come with precisely one heart. The turn and river both bring hearts and you have completed a *backdoor* flush.

> **NOTE: A 'backdoor' hand is one that is completed by receiving favourable cards on both the turn and the river.**

Let's see how likely each of these is:

1) Three hearts on the flop: the chance of this is 0.0084 – a little less than 1% or 118-to-1.

2) Two hearts on the flop: the chance of this is 0.011 – slightly over 10% or approximately 8-to-1. However, you still need to make the flush with a further heart and the chance of this is 0.35, i.e. 35% or approximately 2-to-1. We need to multiply these two probabilities together and this gives a result of 0.0385, roughly 4% or 24-to-1.

3) One heart on the flop: the chance of this is 0.41. You then need to hit consecutive hearts and the chance of this is 0.041. Again we need to multiply these together and this gives 0.017.

Now we add all three up: 0.0084 + 0.0385 + 0.017 = 0.0639. This is 6.4% and is nearly 16-to-1. In fact this estimate is even rather generous because if you consider case '3' we are assuming that you will always play your hand to the river if you have two flush cards and only receive one matching suit card on the flop. You will not – most of the time you will be folding on the flop because the remote chance of the backdoor flush will not justify contributing further bets to the pot. A more realistic figure for the chance of completing a flush is somewhere around 18-to-1 or 19-to-1.

This sobering statistic reveals why playing cards solely for their suitedness is such bad business in hold'em – your flush will come in only slightly more often than one time in 20. The pot you win in that case will nowhere near compensate for all the money that has dribbled away on the other occasions when the flush failed to materialise.

When is Suitedness Useful?

Before discussing the above question I need to explain what is meant by the term 'pot equity'.

Pot Equity

At any particular point of a hold'em deal there is a certain amount of money in the pot, and your hand has a certain chance of winning. Combining these two figures generates your *pot equity*. For example, there is $22 in the pot on the turn and you have a completely unbeatable hand. Your opponent(s) is/are drawing dead and so your pot equity is 100% – which in this case is $22. Another example: you are heads up on the turn and there is $40 in the pot. You have the best hand but your opponent has a 3-to-1 chance to outdraw you. Your pot equity is now 75% – which in this case is $30.

Few Opponents

If you are playing a powerful high card hand then being suited adds just a little extra, but you are basically playing your hand for its high card value. For example, let's say you are playing a $20-$40 game. You have A♥-J♦, open with a raise and end up playing heads up against the small blind who has K♣-Q♠. You have both put $40 into the pot and the big blind contributed $20 (and has folded), so the pot contains $100.

If this hand is played out to the river you will win 60% of the time and your pot equity is thus $60. If we now substitute A♥-J♥, giving you a suited combination your edge now increases slightly and you will emerge on top 62% of the time. Your pot equity has now gone up from $60 to $62. This is an increase of about 3% and as such is not very significant.

Many Opponents

Now let's assume that you are again playing a $20-$40 game but this time have seen the flop cheaply with four opponents including the two blinds. You hold Q♣-10♥ and your four opponents hold the following hands: A♥-8♥, 3♠-3♦, K♥-J♦ and 9♠-8♦. You have all paid $20 so the pot again stands at $100. If this hand is played out to the river then you will win 20% of the time. Thus your pot equity is $20. Now let's change your hand to Q♣-10♣, again making your hand suited. Suddenly your chance of winning the pot improves dramatically. If the pot is played out to the river you will now win 25% of the time, so your pot equity increases from $20 to $25. This is an increase of 25% and makes a huge difference.

Do not make the mistake of thinking that an improvement from 20% to 25% represents just a 5% increase. In absolute terms it does, but what we are interested in here is the *relative* improvement. If you were getting paid $20 per hour for a job and you are now getting $25, that represents a pay rise of 25%.

 TIP: You can make these pot equity calculations at www.twodimes.net/poker/

The value of being suited should now be clear. If you have a big hand with few opponents it is a minor consideration. However, if you have many opponents it makes a huge difference. You will notice that in the latter example, playing your unsuited cards merely gave you value for your bet – you had contributed $20 to the pot and your pot equity was $20. Your bet had neither positive nor negative expectation – it was just a fair bet. However, when your cards become suited suddenly your pot equity leaps to $25 and your bet yields a positive expectation. Generating small edges such as this is what limit hold'em is all about.

Entering the Pot

There are three basic ways that the play can come to you in the pre-flop betting round:

1) No-one has yet entered the pot.

2) One or more players have called (limped).

3) Someone has opened with a raise (and there may be callers)

Let's consider each in turn.

1) No-one has yet entered the Pot

Everyone in the hand so far has folded and the action comes to you. As we know you have a choice here – you can open with a raise, you can just call (limp) or you can fold. Which you will want to do depends on the strength of your hand and your position. When you have a very strong hand, such as a big pair or two very high cards, you will want to open with a raise. This forces other players (with the exception of the blinds) to pay a double bet to stay in the pot. If you just limp then it becomes cheap for players to see the flop with weaker hands and one of them might get lucky and outdraw you. If you have a big hand and other players want to play their speculative hands, then you must charge them a premium to do so.

There is a further reason why you usually want to open with a raise – it gives you a chance to win the pot immediately. Raising puts pressure on the opposition. If everyone folds you win the pot at once (winning the blind money). This is rarely a bad thing. If you limp there are two problems: firstly, it is cheaper for other players to compete; secondly, the small blind (who is already *half in*) can get a cheap look at the flop, while the big blind gets a completely free look at the flop.

Situations where you consider limping are where you have a moderate hand which has the potential to become very good but needs a helpful flop. In such cases you are hoping to see the flop cheaply and actually welcome the participation of other players. Firstly, it boosts the pot size and secondly, if you do get lucky and make a big hand you want someone else to make a decent – but second-best hand – and *pay you off*.

If you are in late or even middle position then you should not open limp. You are less worried about there being a monster hand out against you, and you want to maximise your chances of winning at once. The possibility of winning immediately is such an important consideration that if you want to play from middle or late position it is best to raise.

 TIP: Limping will encourage the participation of other players and may create a multi-way pot. Raising will keep the numbers down.

2) One or More Players have called (limped)

If you are going to play and other players have already entered the pot, then you can raise or just limp along with everyone else. Players who have limped into the pot generally have moderate hands, so if you have a powerful hand you should raise and the others will probably call. Now your powerful hand will have less chance of standing up than if you had been in a position to open raise with it and drive these other players out. However, with more players there will be more money in the middle, so when you do win (and this will be often) you will take down a big pot.

If you have a moderate hand with good drawing possibilities, this is a good time to join in the limping. You will want to hit the flop hard so that you are not really worried about your hand being dominated. For example if you call after two or three limpers with J♠-10♠ there is a serious danger that you are dominated by one or maybe even two other players. However, you are not really looking to make a pair and have it hold up with a hand like this. That can happen, but basically you are after bigger fish. You are hoping to flop a straight or flush draw and make a lot of money if it comes in.

3) Someone has opened with a Raise

If an early position player opens with a raise you need a major hand to compete. If you have such a hand and you want to play, then you will usually re-raise. Many weak players do not understand this principle and you will see them calling pre-flop raises with all sorts of hands, some very good, some relatively weak.

If you think about this, it is obvious why you should raise or fold. Someone has opened with a raise. If they are a sensible player then clearly they should have a strong hand. Now:

1) Your Hand is Weaker

If your hand is likely to be weaker than your opponent's, you should fold. You have no idea how many other players will join in (if any) so you cannot judge whether you have any implied odds. Paying a lot of money to compete against a stronger hand is not smart poker.

2) Your Hand is Stronger

If you really think your hand is stronger then it is quite likely that your hand dominates that of the raiser (e.g. they have A-J and you have A-K). Now your ideal scenario is to take on the raiser heads up, when you will be in an excellent position. Your hand might even hold up if it doesn't improve – a scenario which is most unlikely if there are more players involved. Re-raising creates a good chance to generate this situation. Now other players will have to pay three bets to play (slightly less for the blinds) and they are liable to shy away unless they have a serious hand. You are in a good position and you do not want other drawing hands coming along and confusing the issue.

If a middle or late position player opens with a raise, then the situation is slightly different. Such players do not need such a good hand to open with, and so you can loosen your requirements for taking them on. However, again – if you want to play you should usually raise. The reasons you took on an early raiser with a re-raise still apply here.

An exception to this raising strategy occurs when there has been an open raise and one or more calls. Now you might be able to get good value with a call for a decent drawing hand such as 8-8 or K-Q suited.

 TIP: If you see a player who is often calling raises pre-flop, then they are almost certainly a weak player.

Playing from the Blinds

Any time that you are playing from one of the blind positions, your requirements to enter the pot again change. You have already contributed some money to the pot, so it is less expensive for you to now get involved than for other players. This means that your pot odds (and implied odds) will always be better, and this allows you to take more chances with speculative hands in these positions.

This is especially true of the big blind. If there is no raise before the play gets to you then you can take a free play. If there is a single raise then the pot is likely to be fairly big, and you will only have to contribute one bet rather than two to see the flop.

The small blind is slightly less well placed to take advantage of these factors. Firstly the small blind is (usually) only half a bet, so even with no raises you are still obliged to contribute something to the pot to see the flop. If there has already been a raise then you have to pay 1½ bets, which is 75% of what late position players are paying. Note that as the small blind you are also stuck with the worst possible position for the entire hand.

In summary, if you are in the big blind you can play a fair number of speculative hands against a raiser. This is especially the case if there have also been callers to bump up the pot and thus improve your odds. In the small blind it will be so cheap to see the flop in an unraised pot that you can call with even quite weak hands (note that players calling instead of raising also implies that the hands out against you are weaker). However, to play against a raiser you still need to possess a very good hand.

Chapter Eight

Pre-Flop Play:
Specific Strategies

- ♣ Playing Pairs
- ♣ Playing Unpaired High Cards
- ♣ Playing Speculative Hands
- ♣ In Practice
- ♣ Exercise Eight

We have now discussed a number of concepts that can arise in hold'em which are relevant to pre-flop play. It is now time to consider how these will lead us to assess and play specific hands in specific positions.

Playing Pairs

Before discussing the play of pocket pairs pre-flop there is one important statistic which you must know. The chance of hitting a set on the flop (i.e. a card of the same rank as your pair arriving on the flop and thus giving you three of a kind) is 7½-to-1. Often when you play a pair, your only realistic chance to win the pot is to flop a set. Since this is something of a longshot, you must often make sure that you are getting reasonable pot odds to play your pair.

Top Pairs (A-A, K-K, Q-Q)

These are the very best hands you can get and they will not come along very often. These holdings are so strong that your position at the table becomes irrelevant. When you pick these up, you will bet, raise and re-raise if possible. They are premium hands. You will (nearly always) be the favourite in the pot and you should charge you opponents the maximum to play. Much of the time you will be dominating your opponent's hands. In fact the only situation where this does not happen is when you hold Q-Q and an opponent has A-K (or if you are unlucky enough to run into an overpair).

With A-A you have the best possible hand and with K-K and Q-Q the chance of someone holding a better hand than you is remote.

What you want to happen

Ideally you would like just one or two opponents seeing the flop with you, with these players paying a premium price to do so. The pot will be a good size and you will be a favourite to win it. Sometimes you will find that you will see the flop with more opponents, maybe four or even five. As long as they have all paid well for the privilege, this is fine for you. You will not win these pots as often as you will with just one or two opponents, but when you do, the pots are likely to be very big.

What you don't want to happen

You do not want to let numerous players see the flop cheaply. This is disastrous. You will have failed to build up a big pot and given yourself the greatest possible chance of being out-drawn. You are less likely to win the pot and, when you do, it is smaller.

Sometimes weaker players like to get fancy with these big hands and play them slowly – limping pre-flop and then maybe even just calling on the flop with the idea of unleashing a big raise on the turn when the bet size doubles. However, limping with these hands pre-flop and allowing other, weaker, hands to see the flop cheaply is a major mistake. You will occasionally land a big pot playing like this, but frequently someone speculating with a drawing hand will outdraw you and you suffer an unnecessary and frustrating loss.

Strong Pairs (J-J, 10-10)

These are also excellent holdings. You will nearly always see the flop with these hands, and very often you will be raising and re-raising with them. It is still highly likely that you have the best hand, but now you are less likely to be dominating opponents. If you have J-J an opponent with A-K, A-Q or K-Q has a playable hand. When you hold 10-10 you can add A-J, K-J and Q-J to the mix of hands which will be playable against yours.

You are also much more likely to see overcards on the flop. As we can see in the table on page 144, with Q-Q you are a favourite to dodge overcards on the flop. However, when your pair drops to 10-10 the chance of avoiding overcards is only 30%.

What you want to happen

As with the top pairs, you would again like to see the flop with a small number of opponents, with them paying a premium. With just one or two opponents you may still hold the best hand even if one overcard arrives on the flop. When you have numerous opponents it is likely that any overcard will leave you in trouble. At the very least it will make the hand harder to play.

What you don't want to happen

Same story as with the top pairs. You do not want to let numerous players see the flop cheaply. In principle you don't mind having many opponents – as long as they are paying well for the privilege. If nothing else you will be getting reasonable implied odds to hit a set, and you could also receive a favourable flop of low cards when your pair still has a good chance to stand up.

Medium Pairs (9-9, 8-8, 7-7)

These are good hands and are often playable. They are nearly always playable if no-one has yet entered the pot or if one or more players have entered the pot, but with calls (suggesting moderate hands) rather than raises (suggesting powerful hands). They are not generally good hands to play if you suspect that other players have strong hands, as they are dominated by higher pairs.

One problem with these hands is that it is very likely that one or more overcards will arrive on the flop, and this can make them difficult to handle with small numbers of opponents (with a large number of opponents you will usually just give up if you don't flop a set and the board is otherwise unhelpful).

What you want to happen

Medium pairs can generally be profitable in two ways:

1) You see the flop with one or perhaps two opponents at most. Normally you will need to open with a raise to make this

happen. Now you have a reasonable chance to win even if your pair does not improve.

2) You see the flop relatively cheaply with numerous opponents. Now you are hoping to flop a set, but you have some chances to win even if you do not.

What you don't want to happen

You do not want to pay a premium price to see the flop with a small number of opponents. You do not want to be in a pot with just one or two opponents if there is strong evidence that one of them has a big hand which might dominate you.

Small Pairs (6-6, 5-5, 4-4, 3-3, 2-2)

Unlike the medium pairs, these hands are only playable in certain circumstances. You should not always enter the pot with them as they are just too weak. It is with small pairs that the concept of implied odds (see page 131) really becomes important. When you play these hands and you do not flop a set there will usually be two and maybe even three overcards. If you have more than one opponent in such circumstances it is unlikely that you will be able to continue.

As we already know, the chances of flopping a set are 7½-to-1. If you relied purely on pot odds, to decide whether you could play a small pair pre-flop, you would almost never enter a pot. It would require that seven opponents had already entered the pot before you and this would be a truly freak occurrence.

These hands rely on implied odds. You look to enter pots cheaply, with reasonable pot odds and then hope to flop a set. If you do then you will have a well-concealed monster hand and a fine chance to win a big pot. In other words – your implied odds will be excellent.

You are generally looking for pot odds of around 4-to-1 or 5-to-1 in a modest-sized pot to be able to play these hands. Thus, in a $5-$10 game if there is $20 in the pot and it costs $5 to call then calling is okay. To get 'value' for your call you would need to guarantee winning around $40 when you hit your set. Nothing is ever certain in poker, but it is reasonable to assume that – on average – you will do better than that.

What you want to happen

Small pairs, like medium pairs, can be profitable in two ways:

1) You see the flop heads up with just one opponent who does not necessarily have a strong hand. Now there is a fair chance that you can win unimproved. If your opponent does not make a pair or any kind of draw on the flop then you may win the pot straightaway. If they call along with a weak drawing hand, then they can miss and your small pair may stand up anyway.

2) You see the flop relatively cheaply with numerous opponents. The more the merrier but ideally at least three. Now you are hoping to flop a set. When you do get lucky you can win a very big pot as the strength of your hand will be well disguised. If you miss the set on the flop then, barring some freak event (e.g. you have 4-4 and the flop is 6-5-3), you are done with the hand and will fold as soon as someone bets. Note that you are not worried about being dominated by a higher pair. Unless you receive an excellent flop you plan to give up anyway.

What you don't want to happen

You do not want to pay a premium price to see the flop with a small number of opponents.

Playing Unpaired High Cards

Unpaired high cards are the bread-and-butter hands at hold'em. You will be dealt a couple of decent high cards a lot more often than you will receive a pair, and most of the time when you are involved in a pot it will be with unpaired high cards. With such hands you are basically hoping to receive a card on board to give you a pair. As you are playing two high cards, it is likely that you will then have top pair with either the best, or a decent, kicker. This is usually a strong hand, especially if you have just one or two opponents.

If your high cards are suited, this is a small but potentially significant bonus. It gives you a modest chance to make a flush and is of most use when you have many opponents. Any time that you make a flush in these circumstances, you can win a big pot.

The value of high cards changes significantly with regard to position. This is because the possibility of domination. You need to be very cautious about playing high cards from early position and need the absolute best hands to do so. Consider a hand such as Q-J. If four or five players have already folded then it is quite reasonable to open with this hand. However, if you are either first or second to speak, you should just fold with this hand as it is easily dominated by A-Q, A-J, K-Q and K-J. It is also facing an uphill struggle against A-K and all big pairs. If you remember the game of 100 (see page 136) then trying to play Q-J in early position is like betting on the number 80 when you have eight or nine opponents – far too risky and, in the long run, unprofitable.

Strong High Card Combinations

These are really just A-K and A-Q. If you are in early position, these are the only non-pair hands that you should definitely play and you should raise with them. A-J and K-Q can just about be labelled 'strong high card combinations' and you can still open raise with these, especially if they are suited. All other high card combinations, e.g. A-10, K-J etc are just too weak and vulnerable to domination.

In middle and late position you can again relax your standards. In middle position you can open raise with A-10 and K-J, and in late position you can add Q-J. Other hands such as K-10 and Q-10 are borderline cases.

What you want to happen

Powerful high cards play much like the big pairs. You want a small number of opponents and you want them paying well to see the flop. If you have A-K and face just one opponent (or even two) you can even win pots when your hand doesn't improve. This is most unlikely with more than two opponents. If you can get heads up with a hand that you are dominating then you are in very good shape.

What you don't want to happen

As usual for the big hands you don't want a number of players seeing the flop cheaply with moderate drawing hands.

Moderate High Card Combinations

These are all hands below A-J and K-Q (it is probably best to regard these as 'crossover' hands – they are just about okay to play in early position and certainly okay in middle position). They are A-10, K-J, Q-J, K-10, Q-10 and J-10. Below this and you are getting into the realms of 'speculative hands'. These moderate high cards are hands that you definitely do not want to play against players who have shown a lot of strength, i.e. open raisers from early or middle position. There is a very great danger you will be dominated. For example, a hand like K-10 is deceptive. It looks like a good couple of high cards, but it is dominated by numerous hands: A-A, K-K, Q-Q, J-J, 10-10, A-K, A-10, K-Q and K-J.

These hands are generally playable in two situations:

1) If you are down to just three or four opponents, i.e. middle to late position, then it is okay to open raise with them. There is a reasonable chance that you have the best hand, and the danger of being up against a bigger hand is counter-balanced by the chance that everyone may fold and you might take the blinds straight away.

2) If there have been a couple of callers it is *often* (not always) okay to call with these hands. There are two other factors that should affect your decision: whether your hand is suited, and your position. These hands play much better in volume pots with good position and – as we have already seen – being suited is a big bonus too.

What you want to happen

You want to take the initiative and play with good position against just one or two opponents. Alternatively you are happy to compete in a multi-way pot if you can get in cheaply. In the latter situation you are greatly helped if your cards are suited and also by having good position.

What you don't want to happen

You do not want to pay a premium price to compete against a very strong hand when there is a great danger of domination.

Speculative Hands

Any holding that does not comprise of two high cards and is not a pair is a speculative hand. In fact, strictly speaking a lot of low to medium pairs are speculative hands too, but I have dealt with them in the 'Playing Pairs' section.

Speculative hands can have three things going for them:

1) High Card Strength
2) Suitedness
3) Connectedness

The more of these features that they have, the better the hand. Let's consider each in turn:

1) High Card Strength

You may be puzzled by this, as I have already said that speculative hands do not contain high cards. However, do not make the mistake of thinking that all hands that do not contain aces and kings are equal. J-10 is a clearly stronger hand than 8-7 – you have a much better chance of your hand holding up if you make just a pair. 8-7 in turn is much better than 5-4, for more or less the same reasons. If you are contemplating getting involved with a speculative hand, then the higher the cards the better.

There is another type of speculative hand that has high card strength – a suited ace. If you play a hand such as A♣-6♣, then you are mainly hoping to get in cheap and win a big pot if you make a flush. However, it is also possible that an ace will come on the flop and this *may* give you the best hand. You have to be very cautious with these A-x hands when you pair the ace, especially if somebody else has got excited about the flop. If they have a decent ace with a good kicker then you are in bad shape.

2) Suitedness

This should be fairly straightforward. Suited cards give you a chance to make a flush and, as such, are obviously a bonus. The benefits that derive from having suited cards were discussed at length in the previous chapter.

3) Connectedness

Connected cards offer you chances to make a straight, and the more connected they are the better. The reason for this should be obvious – there are more possible straights to be made. If you have 7-6 you can make four possible straights which use both cards (10-9-8-7-6, 9-8-7-6-5, 8-7-6-5-4 and 7-6-5-4-3). If you have a gap, e.g. 8-6, this drops to three (10-9-8-7-6, 9-8-7-6-5 and 8-7-6-5-4). With 9-6 and 10-6 the numbers drop to two and one respectively.

Note that the straightening value of cards drops off when they get really low. For example 3-4 can only make three straights using both cards. The straight up to the four doesn't exist. The same applies at the opposite end of the food chain as K-Q and Q-J (for example) are limited in the number of straights which they can make. As you will doubtless have realised, this is no big deal as you are not really playing those cards for their straightening value in the first place.

 NOTE: A combination such as 8-6 or 9-7 is known as a *one-gapper*. As you might expect, 7-4 and 9-6 are *two-gappers*.

Speculative hands can be playable if no-one has shown much strength. They are also sometimes playable from the big blind (and the small blind in unraised pots) if the pot odds are attractive.

 WARNING: You need to be quite choosy about when you play speculative hands. If you pick the right circumstances they offer good value. However, many weak players' eyes light up when they see 7♣-6♣ and they will play this hand in any position at any time. This is a *big* leak.

What you want to happen

With a speculative hand you want to get in cheaply when it looks like there will be a lot of players in the pot. It helps if you have good position.

What you don't want to happen

As usual you don't want to be in two- or three-player pots up against big hands.

In Practice

We have now gone through the theory of pre-flop play, and by now you should have a reasonable idea what you are trying to achieve. Now let's look at some specific examples.

Example 1

You are in early position. The UTG folds and it is up to you. What is your play with the following hands?

a)

Answer: You raise. Your queens are a very strong hand. It is most unlikely that there is a better hand out against you. If someone wants to play with a weak hand like K-J (and players will play such hands) then make them pay.

b)

Answer: You call. You have a reasonable hand which is a little too strong to fold. However, you have no idea how the pot will develop and calling is best. The problem with raising is that a player with a strong hand might re-raise and then you end up playing heads-up, out of position with a moderate hand – not a good situation. If you just call you will probably encourage other players to call. If there is then a subsequent raise that is fine – with a few players in the pot you will have reasonable implied odds to hit your set.

c)

Answer: You fold. This is just too weak and you have no idea how the pot will develop. The pair of nines that you had in 'b' is a much more robust hand.

d)

Answer: You raise. One player has already folded and your hand is just about strong enough to open with a raise.

e)

Answer: You call or raise. This is borderline. You have a strong hand and either play can work well or backfire. If there is a big hand out against you, then you are better off calling so that it doesn't get too expensive. However, if there are a bunch of feeble drawing hands out against you, then you are better off raising so that you either get rid of some of them or force them to pay well to play. Unfortunately you have no prior information about this and so this is a difficult decision.

f)

Answer: You fold. This is just too weak. It is far too easy for someone else to be squashing you and, as usual, you have no idea how the pot will develop. With hands like this you need information about the opposition's hands. You don't have it here.

Example 2

You are in middle position. An early player limps in, as does another middle player. What is your play with the following hands?

a)

Answer: You raise. Your queens are very likely to be the best hand so you want to get more money in the pot and force players to pay if they want to play speculative hands. Your hand is so strong that you do not fear re-raises.

b)

Answer: You call. Your nines are certainly worth playing but it is unlikely that you are dominating the opposition. You are not afraid of a raise behind you.

c)

Answer: You call. Calling is again fine. This will very likely be a multi-way pot, and you have very good implied odds if you can hit your set. Even if there is a raise behind you, the pot will probably end up being contested with five or even more players, so your implied odds are fine.

d)

Answer: You raise. As the other two players have limped, you probably have the best hand. You may or may not be dominating other hands, but it doesn't really matter. You have a good holding and you have good position – you should raise.

e)

Answer: You call. You have a decent speculative hand. It is not strong enough to raise, but it is fine for a call. A raise behind you would not be great news, but this is likely to be a multi-way pot and so your good speculative hand is fine to play.

f)

Answer: You fold. You have a modest speculative hand, so calling is not terrible, but folding is best. The trouble is that there are several players yet to enter the pot who may have good hands and may raise and even re-raise. You would be perfectly happy to see the flop for one bet, but you cannot guarantee that here. In 'e' you held Q♣-J♣ which is a much stronger hand and can stand a raise more easily than 10♣-8♣.

Example 3

You are in the cut-off seat. An early player raises and a middle player calls. What is your play with the following hands?

a)

Answer: You re-raise. If you are up against A-A or K-K then it is just not your day. It is likely that your hand is the best right now, and you want to get the button and blinds out of the pot.

b)

Answer: You call. This is a tricky one. There is more danger that you are dominated by a higher pair, but it is quite possible that your opponents have just high cards or even lower pairs. Raising is not bad, but a simple call is probably better.

c)

Answer: You fold. This hand is too weak and has no chance to stand up if you don't hit a set. With only two players definitely in the pot you don't have pot odds, and there is no guarantee that the button and/or blinds will play to give you the value you need.

d)

Answer: You fold. This is a decent drawing hand, but it is no good against an early raiser as you are too likely to be dominated.

e)

Answer: You fold. This is not a trick question. You have a much weaker hand than in 'd' so this is a clear fold. Calling here is a horrible play (which, incidentally, is made by many weak players).

f)

Answer: You fold. You have a reasonable high card hand, but it is very much more likely that you are dominated than vice versa. This hand is just not playable against a sensible early raiser, and there is also a caller to worry about.

Example 4

You are on the button. It is folded round to the cut-off who raises. What is your play with the following hands?

a)

Answer: You re-raise. A raise from the cut-off is less frightening than a raise from an early player. Your 9-9 is a strong hand here but is vulnerable to overcards once the flop comes. Therefore you would very much like to get the blinds out, especially if they have hands like J-10. Your 9-9 is a good hand heads-up but becomes increasingly vulnerable with more players.

b)

Answer: You fold. Your hand is too weak to raise and you cannot call as you have nowhere near the right odds to flop a set.

c)

Answer: You re-raise. This is slightly risky, but if you are going to play the hand you really want to re-raise. There is a very good chance that you have the best hand and, as usual, you would like to get the blinds out.

d)

Answer: You fold. This hand is a bit too weak to get involved with even against a late position raiser.

Example 5

You are in the big blind. A middle player limps as does a late player. The button raises and the small blind calls. What is your play with the following hands?

a)

Answer: You re-raise. You probably have the best hand and it would be very helpful to get rid of either or both of those early limpers. By re-raising you force them to pay two more bets to play and they may decide against it. Calling is rather feeble. Imagine that the limpers have A♥-10♣ and K♦-J♦, the button has 10♠-10♥ and the small blind has Q♣-J♣. You can see that if you force the limpers to fold, then your hand is squashing the other two. If you let the limpers hang around any ace or king on the flop is going to scupper you. I appreciate that this particular situation is rather contrived, but the principle should be clear.

b)

Answer: You call. There is no reason to raise but you are receiving fantastic odds to hit your set.

c)

Answer: You call. This is definitely worth a call, although you will have to be cautious post-flop if you make a pair. If you pair the ace, the button could easily have a big ace and you could be out-kicked. If you pair the nine you may well still be behind against the button (he could have 10-10 or better). What you really want is to hit a flush draw, and you have excellent odds here.

d)

Answer: You call. Your hand is nothing much to write home about, but you will have pot odds of around 9-to-1. This is certainly worth a call with a reasonable speculative hand.

Exercise Eight

(Answers on page 258.)

1) You are in middle position, three off the button, and it is folded round to you. How do you play the following hands?

a)   b)

c)   d)

e) 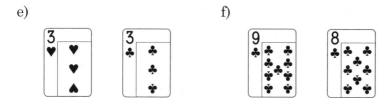 f)

2) You are on the button. An early player limps, a middle player also limps, as does the cut-off. How do you play the following hands?

a)   b)

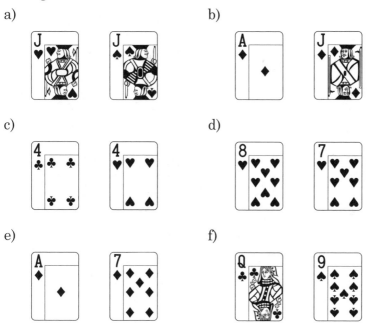

c)   d)

e)   f)

3) You are in the small blind. A middle player raises and the cut-off and button both call. How do you play the following hands?

a)   b)

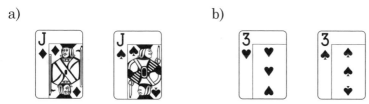

c) 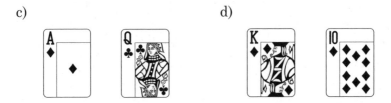 d)

4) You are in middle position. An early player limps and a middle player calls. How do you play the following hands?

a) 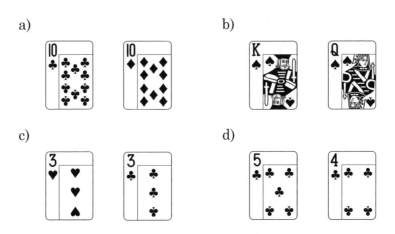 b)

c) d)

Chapter Nine

Post-Flop Concepts

- ♣ Introduction
- ♣ Pre- and Post-Flop Play
- ♣ Aggression
- ♣ Assessing the Flop
- ♣ Betting Concepts

Introduction

If you have read through the previous material and understood it, then you are by now about 75% of the way towards being a decent player at the low limits. If you are playing a $1-$2 game or a $2-$4 game and you can play well at the pre-flop stage then – even if your post-flop play is poor – you are probably going to be at least a break-even player. However, your post-flop play is not going to be poor. In this section we are going to look at how you handle your cards once the flop arrives and how to play the turn and the river.

Pre- and Post-Flop Play

Hold'em divides quite neatly into pre- and post-flop play in a manner similar to how bridge divides into the auction and the play of the hand. In bridge the auction is susceptible (within reason) to exact analysis in much the same way that pre-flop hold'em play can be analysed in great technical detail. Anyone so inclined can memorise tables which denote the 'correct' play in virtually all situations. Many books offer readers such tables and imply that memorising them will lead to perfect pre-flop play. I have chosen not to do this in this book, as I believe that understanding what you are trying to achieve pre-flop is of more relevance than learning tables.

Once the flop appears a similar situation arises to when the auction is complete in bridge and the play of the cards begins. You can still find strong technical players, but there is now much more room for imagination and making plays. It is fairly common to come across hold'em players who have horrible pre-flop standards (and are thus constantly handicapping themselves in their games) but nevertheless actually play rather well after the flop. They have a good feel for what is going on and understand what they and the other players at the table are trying to do.

The Flop and the Turn

Most books make a clear distinction between flop and turn play and discuss them more or less separately. However, I am not sure this is the best way to consider the play in hold'em as the two are very closely related. I think it makes more sense to break up the play into the following three sections: pre-flop play; flop and turn play; and finally river play.

This seems to me to be more logical. The three sections break down (crudely) as follows.

The Play of a Hold'em Hand

1) Pre-flop play decides whether you are going to get involved in the hand or not.

2) Flop and turn play dictates how the deal plays out when everyone still has chances to improve their hands.

3) River play is rather different in that all the cards are now out and you either have the best hand or you don't.

Furthermore, it is quite common to make a play on the flop in order to prepare a particular play on the turn. This is another reason for considering the two rounds together. However, there are two important distinctions between flop and turn play.

Distinctions Between Flop and Turn Play

1) The bet size on the turn doubles. As we know, in a $5-$10 game the betting unit on the flop is $5, increasing to $10 for the turn (and river).

2) When the flop arrives you have two further chances to improve your hand; after the turn just one remains. This makes pot odds calculations very different.

The Arrival of the Flop

The arrival of the flop is really the key moment in a hold'em hand. You already know your two cards and now, in one fell swoop, three of the five board cards arrive. Thus, pre-flop you knew two of the final seven cards (29%). Now you know five of the final seven cards (71%). This is a huge increase in information.

The value of a hand changes dramatically when the three boards cards come down. Hands which were very strong pre-flop can suddenly be left looking rather feeble, while modest pre-flop holdings can turn into monsters. Being able to judge where you stand in a hand at this point is a key skill in hold'em.

The arrival of the flop can be a very frustrating time as it is a sad fact that most flops miss most hands. Many players play perfectly well pre-flop but become enveloped by a fog when the flop comes down. They have waited a long time to pick up a decent hand and now they have one and they have pushed it hard pre-flop. They are now in the mood for a fight and they are not going to let a few lousy board cards dampen their enthusiasm. No sir. Sometimes it can be possible to push hands hard which have missed the flop but doing so blindly is a recipe for disaster.

Having said that, it must be emphasized that when you have what appears to you to be good hand you *must* play actively.

Aggression

All good poker players play actively. Some are merely aggressive, others are very aggressive and some are super-aggressive. One thing you won't hear people saying about a world champion player is: 'Boy, is he good – he really creates problems for his opponents by being cautious at just the right time.'

In poker, as in life, if you want to be successful you have to make things happen for you. This is done by taking the initiative in pots: betting and raising rather than checking and calling. In post-flop play (and pre-flop for that matter), it is absolutely crucial that you play aggressively. There is no winning style of play that relies on passively responding to your opponents' play.

Getting Paid

Limit hold'em is – at heart – a rather technical game. Those of you whose main exposure to poker is via Hollywood films may regard the game as a tremendous battle of egos, where winners can triumph by sheer force of personality. If you are competing live in a major tournament playing no-limit hold'em then there is an element of this in the play. In no-limit hold'em you can bet any amount of money at any time. This means that it is possible to run huge bluffs and bully weak opponents. However, in an anonymous online limit hold'em game such factors are almost completely irrelevant. The amount you can bet at any point in the hand is fixed and so the possibility of shoving all your chips into the pot whilst eyeballing your opponent is not open to you.

Why do better players beat weaker players at limit hold'em? There are many possible answers but there are two very key reasons:

Why Better Players win at Limit Hold'em

1) They win more money with their winning hands.

2) They lose less money with their losing hands.

That's it. That's more or less all there is to it. When a good player has a good hand they know how to push it hard and extract the maximum from their good cards. When they have a good hand but someone else has a better one, they can see the danger and avoid losing as much as a weaker player will.

Why do better players win more money?

1) How do good players win more money with their good hands? They bet and they raise.

2) What do weaker players do that costs them money? They check and they call.

Sometimes it is the correct strategy to check and call. However, this is not very often. If you have a good hand then you should be betting and raising. I cannot emphasize this enough. Even if you play badly, but aggressively, it is very much harder for players to beat you than if you play badly but passively.

When strong limit hold'em players are eyeing up games, what really makes them salivate are players who play passively. Such players are easy to push around. When they hold good hands they let you come along cheaply so that you have chances to outdraw them, and when they have bad hands they happily come along, calling your bets and hoping that something will turn up. Make sure you do not play like this – it is a foolproof strategy for being a loser.

 WARNING: There are some games where it is possible to win playing a conservative strategy: you can win a tennis match from the baseline and you can have a successful football team that is based on a rock-solid defence. You _cannot_ do this in poker. You simply cannot be a long-term winner if you play a safety-first game. It is not possible.

Assessing the Flop

When considering pre-flop play there are usually specific solutions to specific problems. When you have a decent grasp of the principles involved then the correct play in different situations becomes fairly clear. You have just two cards and your opponents have just two cards. They have either bet them or they haven't. With some experience you can get a good handle on how strong your hand is vis à vis the competition.

Post-flop play is much more slippery. Suddenly there are a lot more variables to consider and a lot more questions that need asking. Pre-flop you are really only asking one question: 'Do I belong in this pot?' When the flop comes you need to consider:

Flop Questions

1) How good is this flop for me?

2) Is it likely to be good for other players?

3) If it is good, should I bet and/or raise or should I just call?

4) If I have a little something but suspect other players have better hands, then do I have pot odds/implied odds to play?

5) If it is bad, can I justify hanging around or should I just give up?

6) How many opponents do I have, and is that good or bad?

You also need to remember how players (including you) entered the pot in the pre-flop round.

What happened Pre-flop?

1) Did they bet and/or raise – implying strong holdings?

2) Did they limp – implying weak holdings?

3) Did they open the betting – implying a solid hand?

4) Did they only join in when one or more others had already called – possibly implying more speculative holdings?

5) Did they get a free/cheap play from the blinds – now they could hold absolutely any cards?

6) Did I show strength pre-flop – will players expect me to have a good hand?

That's a lot to think about and there is no straightforward A-B-C way to play. For the moment we will just look at some flops and decide how well they coordinate with our cards and where we think we might stand. For the moment we will not worry about how we will bet the hands (if at all). We just want to assess the impact of the flop. We will worry about the betting later.

Example 1

You are on the button with K♥-K♠. A middle player limps and the cut-off calls. You raise, the big blind calls, as do the middle player and the cut-off. Four of you see the flop. Let's now judge the following flops.

1a)

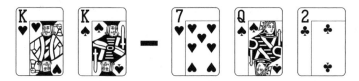

This is a great flop. You have an overpair and the flop is completely uncoordinated. It is very difficult for someone to have a stronger hand than you – the only likely holdings to achieve this are 7-7 and 2-2. Furthermore, players who might want to continue do not have many outs against you. Hands like Q-J and 8-7 are playing five outs, whereas something like 3-3 has just two. You can play this hand confidently.

You are not really worried about having many opponents here. It is so difficult for someone to have a better hand than you.

1b)

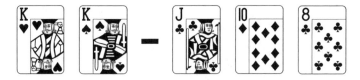

This is a dangerous flop. The three board cards are very coordinated and there is also a two-flush. You should still have the best hand but it is not out of the question that you are already behind. Your opponents were all limping pre-flop, so hands like J-10 and 10-8 are possible. Furthermore, hands that have connected with the flop suddenly have an awful lot more outs against you than in '1a'. For example, 10♥-9♥ has 13 outs, Q♦-J♥ has 9 outs and A♣-5♣ has 12 outs. Proceed cautiously.

This is a flop where you would very much like to have as few opponents as possible. Just one other player could easily miss this flop, but as more players are in the pot it becomes increasingly likely that someone has got a good piece of it.

1c)

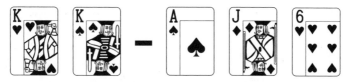

This is a bad flop. If someone has just an ace in their hand you are playing just two outs. Of course you have no way of knowing if there is an ace out against you, but the fact that there might be acts as a brake on your ambitions. If you bet and war breaks out you will have to fold. If you bet and other players come along for the ride you will be faced with difficult decisions.

Example 2

An early player opens with a raise and a middle player calls. The button also calls, as does the small blind. You are in the big blind with Q♠-10♠ and – with pot odds of 9-to-1 – make a perfectly reasonable call. Five of you see the flop.

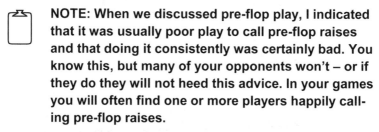

NOTE: When we discussed pre-flop play, I indicated that it was usually poor play to call pre-flop raises and that doing it consistently was certainly bad. You know this, but many of your opponents won't – or if they do they will not heed this advice. In your games you will often find one or more players happily calling pre-flop raises.

2a)

This is a fantastic flop. You have top two pair and are in great shape. You have even overtaken the early raiser if they were playing A-A or K-K. If someone has A-Q or K-Q they have what appears to them to be a very good hand, but in reality they have just three outs against you. Your main worry is that another high card will appear which could allow someone to overtake you. For example, a jack means that Q-J and A-K (straight) now beat you, whereas a king or ace leaves you vulnerable to straights while someone with two pair using high cards now has a better two pair than you.

2b)

This is a pretty decent flop. You have an open-ended straight draw, giving you eight good outs. You also have a small chance to make a flush as there is one spade on the board. Finally you have an overcard, but I wouldn't get too excited about this. There was an early raiser and a couple of callers, so there are some good hands out there. The main value of your hand is with the straight draw.

2c)

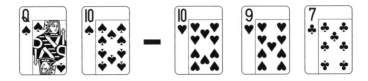

You have top pair, good kicker which is often a very strong hand. Here, however, it is not worth a great deal. The pre-flop raiser may well have an overpair to the board, and any number of the three callers could also find this board attractive. You are badly behind against hands such as K-10 and A-10. Furthermore, the board is rather coordinated with the 7, 9 and 10 all within touching distance, making straight draws possible. Finally, there is a two-flush which also harms your chances. This is the kind of flop where the winning hand is likely to be more than just a pair. Although you have caught the flop to the extent that you have made top pair, your hand does not coordinate well with the flop for the purpose of making better hands such as straights and flushes.

With a flop like this, the number of opponents you have is critical. If you had just one opponent (for example there is a raise from a middle position player, everyone folds and you call from the big blind), then your hand is looking pretty good. They might have caught a good piece of the flop but then again they might not have. However, as the number of opponents increases, so does the danger that this flop poses.

2d)

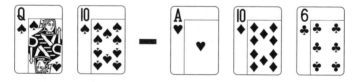

This is the kind of flop that encourages weak players to dribble away their money. With four opponents, all of whom should have decent hands, this second pair hand is worth very little. If someone has A-A, 10-10 or A-10 you have no outs at all. However, even more modest holdings give you few reasons to be cheerful. A-K and A-J leave you with five outs, while A-Q leaves you trying to hit two outs (the missing tens). This is a decent-sized pot and you might think it is worth hanging around to try and improve, but there is a further problem in that even a queen might not make you a winning hand (it won't if an opponent has A-Q, K-J or even Q-Q (the last being, admittedly, unlikely). I know your opponents can't have everything, but they will turn up with such hands more often than you expect. Chasing outs that merely give other players even bigger hands than you is not the way to play good poker.

 TIP: Whenever you play a speculative hand against a number of opponents who have shown strength, you are really looking to make more than just a pair. You won't do this very often, which is precisely why they are speculative hands.

Example 3

You are UTG holding A♥-J♣ and you open with a raise. Everyone folds round to the blinds and they both call. Three of you see the flop.

3a)

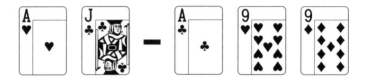

This is certainly not a bad flop. You have top pair, good kicker and only two opponents. However, there is a subtle problem with this hand – it is unlikely to make you any money. You have shown strength pre-flop, so your opponents will regard it as likely that you have an ace. So what kind of hand is going to give you action?

Someone with an ace and a weak kicker may elect to come along, but they are not going to get frisky with their hand. Also, note that if a king, queen or nine happens to land on the board then your lovely jack kicker will no longer play and you will split the pot with someone playing a feeble A-2.

Someone with a nine is going to get involved. Unfortunately, they are beating you and you are playing just two outs against such a hand.

The most likely result here is that you bet the flop and everyone folds. Not a bad result certainly, but if someone comes along with you then your hand is not that exciting.

3b)

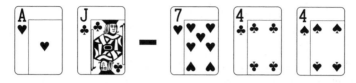

The flop has completely missed you but, considering that it has, it is about as good as could be hoped for. It is quite likely that this raggedy collection missed everyone else too. You can still bet your hand confidently. If somebody has a four you are, of course, in big trouble. However, even if an opponent has a seven or is playing a small pair, you still have six outs and a reasonable chance to make a better hand by the river.

3c)

The flop has again completely missed you, and this time there is no good news. The flop is high-ish, moderately connected, and it is likely that one of the blinds has got a piece of this. The queen is bad news, as if an opponent has paired the queen then your only out is with an ace. The two-flush also hurts you. You don't even have the benefit of a gutshot draw to generate a few extra outs against a better hand. This is just a mess.

Betting Concepts

Now we have some experience of assessing how our hand has connected with the flop, we need to consider how we will play the hand on the flop and beyond. To do this we need to bet our hand successfully.

The Language of Poker

Betting is the language of poker. Every time someone makes a bet (or indeed a check or a call) they are essentially saying something about their hand. Your job, as a poker player, is to interpret this language and act accordingly. However, this is not a universal language – everyone will speak a slightly different dialect. Weak players are generally easy to interpret. When a weak player makes a strong play (betting or raising) it generally means one of the following:

1) 'I have a strong hand.'
2) 'I think my hand is the best right now.'

When a tough player makes a strong play it can take on a much wider range of meanings. As well as...

1) 'I have a strong hand.'
2) 'I think my hand is the best right now.'

... he might also be saying...

3) 'I want you to *think* I have a strong hand.'
4) 'I think *you* have a weak hand.'
5) 'I have very good chances to make the best hand.'

or even...

6) 'I am going to bully you. Are you going to stand up to me?'

However, before you can start to interpret your opponents' betting you need to be aware of the basic strategies for playing hands post-flop. These are: the free card, betting, raising and check-raising.

The Free Card

There may be no such thing as a free lunch, but free cards certainly exist, and they are a key component of poker. A free card is any card you get, either on the turn or river, for which you do not have to 'pay' a bet. If you currently hold the better/best hand, then giving a free card is bad news – you are effectively giving your opponent(s) infinite pot odds. Conversely, if you are behind in a pot and receive a free card, this is very good news. You are now the happy punter in receipt of infinite pot odds.

The idea of a free card is closely tied in with the idea of 'protection'. If you hold what is currently the best hand and you bet (or raise), you force other players to pay to get to the river. By doing so, you are 'protecting' your hand. If you do not bet/raise at appropriate moments, then your opponents will receive free/cheap cards and you will have failed to protect your hand.

 TIP: Strong players absolutely loathe giving free cards and will do anything to avoid it. Weak players give them all over the place.

Look back at the section 'What happens with good position' (see page 134). We can now interpret the play here in a different way. With good position the player was able to protect his hand and he won the pot. When he had bad position and failed to protect his hand he gave a free card and this led to his downfall.

It might seem strange to introduce the idea of a free card before discussing betting. However, in a sense, the purpose of most bets is to avoid giving free cards. Furthermore, as we shall see, sometimes you need to bet (or raise) in order to obtain free cards.

Betting

When you think you have the best hand, you should nearly always bet. This may seem blindingly obvious, but you would be surprised how many players, especially at low limits, are content to check and call with good hands and hope that their opponents will 'bet their hands for them'. Betting accomplishes various things that checking and calling simply can't:

Reasons to Bet

1) If you do have the best hand you guarantee getting more money into the pot.

2) You avoid giving free cards. If your opponents have drawing hands you force them to pay to try and improve.

3) It is possible that everyone else will fold and you will win the pot at once. This is rarely a bad thing.

4) You obtain information about the opposition's hands. If you check, they bet and you call, you have no idea at all about their hands. They may just have bet because you showed weakness by checking. Then again, they may actually have a good hand. You can't be sure. However, if you bet and they call then they ought to have something. It may not be very much but if they had nothing at all, they would probably have folded.

Raising

As we know, when there has been a bet (and maybe one or more calls) and the play comes to you there is the option of raising. A raise is often made as a pure 'value' play. You think you have the best hand, so you raise to get more money into the pot.

However, raising is also often used as a tactical device, especially on the flop. Before discussing when this can be a strong play, we need to consider the phenomenon of 'checking to the raiser'.

Checking to the Raiser

A typical occurrence in low-limit games (this is much less the case in middle- and higher-limit games) is that players will 'check to the raiser'. This means that if a player shows strength on a previous round, players having to speak before this player on the subsequent round will 'defer to the authority' of this player by checking.

Here is a typical situation where it can be good to make a tactical raise. Four players see the flop and you are on the button and will be last to speak. Note that you are thus in the best possible position. The first player bets, the next player folds and the third player calls. You have a reasonable hand which you want to play but you cannot be certain that your hand is best.

Now, you could call and see what arrives on the turn, but another play is to raise. Note that this is the flop round so the extra cost (compared to calling) is only one small bet. Now if both your opponents are compliant they will just call your raise (rather than re-raising) and then check to you when the turn card comes.

Now you are in a good position. If you do not like the look of the turn card then you can check and take a free card. Note that this is not, strictly speaking, a free card. You created the possibility of making this play with a raise on the flop. That cost you an extra small bet. However, you have now saved yourself one big bet, for a net gain of one small bet.

However, if the turn card looks promising (it may not necessarily have to help you for this to be the case – it may just appear likely that it has not helped your opponents), you have the option of betting.

By raising on the flop (and not being reraised) you have taken control of the hand and the other players are dancing to your tune.

Check-Raising

A check-raise occurs when a player initially checks on the betting round and then subsequently raises in response to a bet. If you have a strong hand and you are in early position then this is a tactic well worth considering. If you feel fairly sure that someone will bet – allowing you to check-raise – then this is usually the best play. There are two reasons for this:

Reasons to check-raise

1) You get extra money into the pot.

2) Anyone holding a drawing hand now has to call two bets instead of one bet and thus their pot odds are much worse.

However, the drawback of attempting a check-raise is that no-one may bet and you will have allowed the dreaded free card.

Pot Odds (again)

When you are involved in a pot you will often (sadly enough) come to the conclusion that you do not currently hold the best hand. If your hand appears to be well beaten then you will fold. However, as we saw in the preceding chapters, there are often quite good chances for weaker hands to improve to winning hands by hitting their outs. Whether you now have a profitable strategy of sticking around and seeing if this will happen depend on the pot odds.

Now that we have considered the factors that affect post-flop play, we need to move on to specific strategies as to how to play our hands.

Chapter Ten

Post-Flop Strategy

- ♣ **When to Raise**
- ♣ **The Importance of Position**
- ♣ **Outs and Pot Odds**
- ♣ **Playing a Strong Draw**
- ♣ **Slowplaying**
- ♣ **Staying out of Trouble**
- ♣ **River Play**
- ♣ **Putting it all Together**

The previous chapter was rather theoretical. Now let's look at some practical examples that demonstrate how these concepts are applied in actual hands. In all of these examples we will assume that you are playing in a $2-$4 game where the small is $1 and the big blind is $2.

In the following examples we will see all of the earlier ideas coming into play. We will follow the thought processes of a competent hold'em player as they decide what to do in various situations.

Hold'em is a complex game and there are hundreds of possible combinations of your hand, your opponents' hands, the board, the pre-flop play, the size of the pot etc. It is impossible to pre-pare for all eventualities. Hold'em is a game where experience counts a great deal. When you start playing you probably won't have much of a feel for what you are trying to do, unless you are a very natural, instinctive card player.

In this chapter I am going to give you a head start by demon-strating some basic plays and also by giving you an idea of the kinds of things you should be thinking about during a hand.

I am not going to provide specific guidelines such as: 'if you flop top pair with a good kicker and there is a bet before you, you should do such and such,' or 'if you flop middle pair and it is checked to you, you should ... etc.' I don't think such advice is particularly helpful. Poker is highly situational and quite sub-tle factors can affect your decisions. What I am going to do is guide you through the kind of thought processes that a compe-tent player would have that would affect their decisions.

When to Raise

When one of your opponents has a good hand but you have a better one, you will want to put in a raise at some point. Where to do this is a tricky decision, but the following examples dem-onstrate the factors that should influence your decision.

Example 1

You are on the button with K♥-K♠ in an online game. A middle player limps and the cut-off calls. You raise, the big blind calls, as do the middle player and the cut-off. There is $17 in the pot and four players. The flop comes as follows:

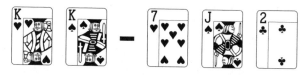

Your first job is to assess the flop. As we noted before, this is a great flop for you. Adopting the principle of checking to the raiser, everyone now checks and – obviously – you bet. The big blind folds but the middle player raises (actually check-raises) and the cut-off folds.

By raising, the middle player is suggesting that he thinks he has the best hand. So, is this likely? If you think about it you will quickly see that it is not. The hands that currently beat you are: A-A and J-J (not likely – he would have raised with these pre-flop), J-7, J-2 and 7-2 (these are very strange hands to play) 7-7 and 2-2 (these are possible). So the only realistic hands to worry about are 7-7 and 2-2. However, there are very many more hands that would look good to him that you are beating, e.g. A-J, K-J, Q-J, J-10, 8-7, 7-6, A-7, A-2 etc.

He has probably made a pair of jacks and thinks he has the best hand. From his point of view this is quite likely. You could easily have raised with something like 9-9, 10-10, A-K, A-Q or even K-Q, and all of these hands would now be losing to his.

You, however, know better. It is almost certain that you have the best hand here, and so you re-raise and you opponent calls. Both you and your opponent have contributed a further three small bets to the pot, adding $12. There is $29 in the pot and two players. The turn brings:

This is a harmless card, often referred to as a blank.

> **NOTE: A blank is a card which arrives on the turn or river and is most unlikely to be of help to any of the players in the pot.**

Your opponent checks and you bet. He calls. Note that the betting unit increases on this round to $4. Thus you have each contributed a further $4, bring the pot to $37. The river brings:

You bet once again and you opponent calls. Your kings take the pot which finally totals $45.

After the river betting was complete, your opponent called your bet and you showed your pair of kings (or rather the software did this for you automatically). In live play you would also have turned over your cards and then if your opponent was beaten (as he was here) he simply mucks his cards. The same thing happens online but with one crucial difference. On virtually all sites it possible to get a hand history which reveals the hole cards of all players who were involved in a showdown. You should always keep an eye on this as it is crucial to see what kind of hands your opponents are calling you with. In this particular example, the hand history shows that your opponent held J♦-10♥ for a pair of jacks.

Raising on the Turn

This all seems rather straightforward and you took down a nice pot. However, there was, in fact, another way you could have played the hand. Let's consider the situation on the flop when the middle player raises you. You worked out that you almost certainly had the best hand and so re-raised, which was quite reasonable. However, there was another way to play the hand which would have been slightly more profitable. Instead of raising, you simply call. Now there is $25 in the pot.

When the turn card arrives it is very likely that your opponent will assume that he is winning and bet. Now you raise. Since your opponent holds top pair he will probably call, bringing the pot to $41. He will then call again when you bet the river and the final pot will be $49 which is $4 more than previously. By waiting until the turn to raise, you have made an extra $2.

This may not sound like much, but reeling in these extra bets is crucial in limit hold'em. One day you will be on the wrong side of this deal, but you will lose $2 less than your opponent did here. The luck will have balanced out, but your skilful play will be showing a $2 profit.

It is because of the possibility of plays such as these that I believe you have to consider flop and turn play together. The call on the flop does not make sense in isolation because you almost certainly have the best hand. However, it is part of a plan which involves raising on the turn.

The Importance of Position

We have already discussed the concept of position both in terms of pre- and post-flop play. When you have bad position you are stuck with it for the whole hand. Conversely when you have good position this benefits you for the whole hand. The following examples show how this can be exploited.

Example 2

This hand is very similar to that from Example 1. This time you are in the small blind again with K♥-K♠. A middle player limps and the cut-off calls. You raise, the big blind calls as do the middle player and the cut-off. There is $17 in the pot and four players. The flop is the same as previously:

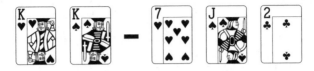

You bet, the big blind folds and the middle player raises. The cut-off folds. All the same arguments as before apply here and so you re-raise. The middle player calls. There is $29 in the pot and two players. The turn again brings:

You bet and the middle player calls. The pot is $37. The river is yet again the same:

You bet and he calls. Since your hands are the same as from the previous example, you again take down a $45 pot.

Out of Position

You may be wondering if it is possible to play this hand more profitably as indeed was the case with Example 1. In order to achieve this you will simply call on the flop when you get raised and then when the turn card arrives you will check, planning a check-raise.

The problem here is that you are out of position and if you check the turn your opponent may be uncooperative and check along after you. Now you can bet the river and he will call, but he has saved himself a whole big bet. Instead of the pot ending up at $49 it ends up at $41. Rather than gaining $2, you have forfeited it.

Notice what has happened. You have been the victim of a

successful free card play. Your opponent raised on the flop, you lost the initiative and ended up giving him a free card. This is typical of what happens when you are playing out of position.

There is one final point here. When the harmless 6♠ arrives on the turn, I suggested that your opponent might check but, actually, this is rather unlikely. From his point of view he may well have the best hand here (you are quite likely to have just overcards with A-K or A-Q) and he would be worried that by checking he is actually giving *you* a free card. Thus in this particular instance your attempt to check-raise the turn will probably be successful. However, note that it is quite possible that a scary card will arrive on the turn, such as an ace, queen or even a king. If this does happen and you play the same way then your opponent is very likely to check. You thus end up winning a smaller pot.

 TIP: When you have a strong hand but are out of position, it is usually best to play it hard.

Example 3

An early player opens with a raise and a middle player calls. The button also calls, as does the small blind. You are in the big blind with Q♠-10♠ and – with pot odds of 9-to-1 – make a perfectly reasonable call. There is $20 in the pot and five players. The flop comes down as follows:

As noted before, this is a wonderful flop for you. The small blind checks. What do you do?

You check, planning a check-raise. The danger with planning a check-raise is that the hand will be checked out and you will give a free card. However, this is not likely here. An early player opened the betting with a raise and there were two callers. Someone should have something.

The early player now bets and the middle player raises. The button and small blind fold. There is $26 in the pot. What do you do?

You re-raise. This is a sort of big check-raise. The early player folds and the middle player calls. There is $34 in the pot and two players. The turn brings:

This is a slightly worrying card, but you should bet again. You do and your opponent calls. There is $42 in the pot.

The river brings:

This is a rather ugly card that puts four to an open-ended straight on board. We shall look at river play in more detail later, but it is best to check here. Your opponent also checks. Unfortunately he has K♣-Q♦ and he has made a better two-pair hand. You have been outdrawn, but notice that your opponent picked up an open-ended straight draw on the turn so he did have a lot of outs against you.

Outs and Pot Odds

Much of the time it will be fairly obvious that you do not currently have the best hand in the pot. Perhaps you started with the best hand pre-flop but the flop has been a bad one for you. Or maybe you played a speculative hand that only connected slightly with the flop. In such cases a consideration of pot odds is crucial to assess whether continuing to play is a profitable proposition.

Example 4

You are on the button with K♥-K♠. A middle player limps and the cut-off calls. You raise, the big blind calls as do the middle player and the cut-off. There is $17 in the pot and four players. The flop comes as follows:

As we saw before this is a very dangerous flop for you. Nevertheless, everybody checks to you. Now you should bet. Even though the flop is scary you should not check – this is a very bad time to give a free card. After you bet the big blind then check-raises and the middle player calls. The cut-off folds. Now you can fold, call or raise. So, what do you do?

You should call. Folding is much too feeble. Although the board is scary, you do have an overpair and it is still quite likely that you have the best hand, though your opponents undoubtedly have a lot of outs against you. Re-raising is not a terrible play but in this particular situation it is over-aggressive. The key point here is that your call *closes the betting*. If you raise you keep the betting open and are then vulnerable to a further re-raise.

There are very many hands that the big blind could hold where he will be a big favourite over you and re-raise, e.g. Q-9, 9-7, J-J, 10-10, 8-8, J-10, J-8, 10-8. When we tried to think of hands that our opponent could have that were beating us in Example 1, we could only come up with 2-2 and 7-7 – nothing else made sense. Here, however, because the board is so coordinated, there are numerous hands that are beating us.

 TIP: When you are concerned that you may not have the best hand and your call will close the betting, this is often the best play.

So, you call. There is $29 in the pot and three players. Now let's consider various different possibilities for the turn card:

Example 4a)

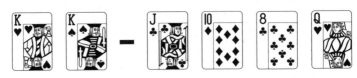

The big blind bets and the middle player calls. There is $37 in the pot. What do you do?

To answer this question we need to go through a quick deductive process.

1) Are we winning?

Most unlikely. We have two opponents and someone (most likely the big blind) probably has a nine. Even if no-one has a nine, someone will have two pair or even a set.

2) So, we will assume that we are not winning. Do we have outs to improve to a winning hand?

Yes, we do. An ace or a nine will complete a straight.

3) Are any of these outs tainted?

Possibly. The A♣ and the 9♣ will put three clubs on the board and the passive, calling play of the middle player suggests that he may be on a flush draw, although we cannot be certain.

4) Do we have pot odds to play?

Yes. There are 46 remaining cards and either six or eight are outs for us. Even if we assume the worst and allow ourselves just six outs, this gives us odds of 40-to-6 or about 7-to-1. The pot odds are 37-to-4 (we need to put $4 into a $37 pot) which is about 9-to-1. We can certainly call.

5) Is there anything else to worry about?

Yes. If someone has A-K, they have made the nut

straight and we will need to hit an ace just to tie. However, this is highly improbable. If the big blind had A-K he would probably not have raised on the flop and if the middle player had A-K he would raise now rather than call.

6) Since we can call, is there any mileage in raising?

No. In principle, when you have decided that you can call it is always good to consider the possibility of raising, but here you will just get re-raised by a player holding a nine and end up with an unprofitable draw.

If you are new to the game of hold'em this may seem terribly complicated but it isn't really. I have deliberately broken the thought process down into numerous steps to clarify it. In reality an experienced player would take about two seconds to think: 'There are four cards to a straight on board ... I'm probably losing ... looks like I could have eight outs ... $37 in the pot, $4 to call ... easy call.'

It is rather like learning to drive. For a learner driver a simple task such as changing gears can seem immensely difficult. There are so many things to remember: ease off the accelerator, depress the clutch, select a gear, change gear, release the clutch, hand back on the steering wheel and so on. All the while there is all the other stuff to worry about: steering, looking in front of you, checking the rear-view mirror, watching for road signs, traffic lights etc. A total nightmare. Put like this it is a wonder anybody ever learns to drive. However, as with all repetitive tasks, after a while control of the car becomes easier and – eventually – it becomes second nature.

Now let's try another scenario.

Example 4b)

We have the same turn card but now after the big blind bets the middle player raises. There is $41 in the pot. What do you do? Well, let's ask the same questions:

1) Are we winning?

No way. The middle player surely has a nine even if the big blind doesn't.

2) So, we will assume that we are not winning. Do we have outs to improve to a winning hand?

Yes, we do. An ace or a nine will complete a straight.

3) Are any of these outs tainted?

Possibly. Someone may have two clubs for a flush draw. However, that doesn't seem all that likely.

4) Do we have pot odds to play?

Let's work it out. Let's be optimistic and assume that we do have eight outs. There are 46 remaining cards which gives us odds of 38-to-8 or about 5-to-1. The pot odds are 41-to-8 (we need to put $8 into a $41 pot) which is also about 5-to-1. So, if this is a valid calculation we have a borderline call.

5) Is there anything else to worry about?

Yes. There is a ton of other stuff to worry about. For a start it looks like there is at least one nine out against us which cuts our pot odds from 38-to-8 to 39-to-7 or possibly even 40-6. This is now pushing up towards 6-to-1 or 7-to-1. Since our call is borderline in the first place, this quickly makes it unprofitable.

Next, there is a danger that someone else has a king too. Then we will only split the pot if we do improve.

Finally, our call does not close the betting. If the big blind has a nine he will re-raise (and there may even be a subsequent cap from the middle player). Action like this will trash our pot odds.

6) So, what should we do?

Fold. Calling is far too risky.

Can you see what has happened here? By raising, the middle player has successfully protected his hand.

Let's try another turn card.

Example 4c)

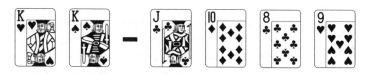

Another ugly card arrives on the turn, putting an open-ended straight on board. The big blind bets and the middle player calls. There is $37 in the pot. What do you do? Same questions again.

1) Are we winning?

Most unlikely. Someone probably has a queen or a seven and two-pair hands are also possible.

2) So, we will assume that we are not winning. Do we have outs to improve to a winning hand?

Yes, we do. A queen will complete a straight. It is vaguely possible that a king will win, but this is not that likely and there are only two of them available anyway.

3) Do we have pot odds to play?

We probably have four outs and there are 46 unseen cards. Our odds are 42-to-4 which is 10½-to-1 and our pot odds are 37-to-4 which is about 9-to-1. We don't quite have the right odds. However, we do have implied odds. If we can hit the queen on the river we should pick up and extra bet or two. This makes the call borderline.

4) Is there anything else to worry about?

Yes. If someone does have a queen it takes away one of our outs and reduces the pot odds to 43-to-3 which is up to 14-to-1. This is nowhere near enough. There is also a slight danger that someone else has a king and we will only tie if we improve.

5) So, what should we do?

Fold. Calling is not terrible but folding is best.

 WARNING: You must be careful with pot odds calculations. Always look for other factors (such as tainted outs and other players holding cards which may result in a tie) which can reduce your odds.

Example 5

An early player limps and a middle player calls. You are on the button with J♠-10♠ and also call as does the small blind. The big blind raises, indicating a strong hand as he could simply have checked and got to see the flop free of charge. Everyone calls so there is $20 in the pot and five players. The flop comes down:

Not a brilliant flop for you but you do have a gutshot draw. The small blind checks and the big blind bets. The early player folds but the middle player calls. There is $24 in the pot. What do you do?

Let's wheel out the usual questions:

1) Are we winning?

Of course not.

2) How many outs do you have?

There are four missing nines which will complete a straight. Our hand has absolutely nothing else going for it. There is almost no chance that a jack or ten will be good enough.

3) Do we have pot odds to play?

Our hand is worth four outs. There are 47 unseen cards so our odds are 43-to-4 which is about 11-to-1. Our pot odds are 24-to-2 which is 12-to-1. We have got pot odds to call.

Note that our implied odds are also good. If the miracle nine does arrive then it will not look that dangerous. We will hold the nut hand and can count on winning a few more bets.

There is an old saying in poker that you should never draw to an inside straight. This is nonsense. It all depends on pot odds. Sometimes it is correct play, sometimes not. There are no hard and fast rules about it.

4) Is there anything else to worry about?

The only very slight concern is that our call does not close the betting. The small blind (who originally checked) is still to play. However, he limped in and then checked the flop. It is most unlikely that he has a hand strong enough to check-raise when there are three other players in the pot.

5) So, what should we do?
Call.

You call and the small blind folds. There is $26 in the pot and three players. The turn now brings:

The big blind bets and the middle player calls. What now?

A quick calculation shows that we still have our four outs from 46 unseen cards, giving us odds of 42-to-4 or 10½-to-1. There is $34 in the pot and it costs $4 to call, so the pots odds are 34-to-4 or 8½-to-1. So this looks like a fold. Right?

Wrong! Look carefully. The ace has created a further possibility as a king will now complete the top straight. This structure where you have chance to make two straights but not with an open-ended draw is known as a *belly-buster*.

So, in fact you have eight outs not four, giving us odds of 38-to-8 which is approximately 5-to-1. You have a very easy call.

You call. There is $38 in the pot and three players. The river brings:

Wonderful. You have hit your straight. The big blind bets and the middle player folds. You have the nut hand and raise. The big blind calls and his two-pair hand A♦-Q♦ loses to your straight. Your alertness on the turn enabled you to pick up a big pot.

Example 6

An early player limps and a middle player calls. You are on the button with K♠-10♠ and also call as does the small blind. The big blind raises, indicating a strong hand as he could simply have checked and got to see the flop free of charge. Everyone calls so there is $20 in the pot and five players. The flop comes:

This is a reasonable result for you. You have a gutshot draw and a small chance to make a flush with running spades. The small blind checks and the big blind bets. The early player folds but the middle player calls. There is $24 in the pot. What do you do?

Let's perform the usual analysis:

1) Are we winning?

Of course not. We only have king high.

2) How many outs do we have?

There are four missing queens which will complete a straight. It is possible that a king will be good but this is far from certain. The big blind may have A-K, or an even stronger hand such as A-A or K-K. The middle player might have K-Q. Furthermore, a king will not be good enough if someone already has a big hand, such as J-J, 9-9 or even J-9. Other holdings such as K-J also cripple the value of our king as an overcard.

In this situation you have four *clean* outs to a queen and you have three outs to a king. However, as we saw in the previous paragraph, it is far from certain that a king is an out. In these circumstances the correct way to assess the value of a king as an out is to downgrade it slightly. Instead of regarding it as three outs, it is reasonable to consider a king as one out. If no-one had shown much strength pre-flop you might consider this to be worth two outs instead. This is not an exact science but it doesn't have to be. You just need to be aware of the possibility and realise that the chance of a king is worth more than zero outs but less than three.

However, you also have a backdoor flush draw and this is worth a little something. The chance of hitting spades on both the turn and river is approximately 24-to-1. It is reasonable to add on something between one and two outs for this possibility.

Thus in total you have about six or seven outs.

3) Do we have pot odds to play?

We have decided that we will assess our hand as being worth seven outs. There are 47 unseen cards so our odds are 40-to-7 or 41-to-6 which is around 6-to-1 or 7-to-1. Our pot odds are 24-to-2 which is 12-to-1. We easily have pot odds to call.

4) Is there anything else to worry about?

Not really.

5) So, what should we do?

Call.

You call, closing the betting. There is $26 in the pot and three players. The turn brings:

This is a teasing card. The big blind bets and the middle player now raises. There is $38 in the pot. What do you do?

Now you have to think about what kind of hand the middle player might be holding. The big blind has shown a great deal of strength in this hand, and yet the middle player is now raising on the expensive street. When a player makes a play like this they will generally have at least a two-pair hand.

I would say that the likelihood here is that the weakest hand that the middle player holds is K-J for the top two pair. There are also hands he can hold that are much stronger, such as J-J, 9-9, 3-3 and Q-10. You are in big trouble against all these hands; if he has the straight you have a mere three outs just to tie the pot; if he has a set you only have four queens to make a straight (remember that a set is an immensely powerful hand – even if a king comes and you improve to trip kings, he will improve to a full house).

It is just about possible that the middle player has a weaker hand with J-9, A-K or K-Q. However, even if he has one of these weaker holdings, he is still beating you and you remain short of outs. For example against K-Q you still have only the missing queens, as making a two-pair hand with a ten will result in a straight for your opponent.

Finally, you still have the big blind to worry about.

So, there is $38 in the pot and it costs you $8 to call. We are not sure how many outs we have so let's turn the question round and ask: 'how many outs do we need?' The pot is offering 38-to-8, which is about 5-to-1. There are 46 unseen cards and in order to have pot odds we need eight outs (to generate odds of 38-to-8). There is almost no chance that we have eight outs, so we should fold.

Once again I have broken down the thought process to make it completely clear. An experienced player will not go to such great lengths. He will realise that the turn raise from the middle player represents a very strong hand, quickly see that his only out is likely to be the queen, and observe that the pot is not offering anywhere near the right odds to chase it.

What if the middle player is bluffing?

When you start out playing hold'em there is a natural inclination to always call opponents to make sure that they really are beating you. Very occasionally, you find that they have been running some huge bluff and that your modest hand is actually best. However, this will not happen very often. A very great percentage of the time a strong play indicates a strong hand.

In the previous example this is even more likely to be the case because (from the middle player's point of view) there are two other players in the pot, one of whom (the big blind) obviously has a very decent hand. In these circumstances it is wildly improbable that the middle player is bluffing.

However, let's change the earlier play so that the hand develops as follows. You again have your K♠-10♠ on the button. The play is passed round to you and you open with a raise. The small blind folds and the big blind calls. The flop is again J♠-9♥-3♦. The big blind checks and you bet, hoping that he will fold but you have some chances to improve anyway. The big blind calls, bringing the pot to $13. The turn again brings J♠-9♥-3♦-K♥. The big blind checks, you bet and now he check-raises. The pot is now $25. Do you still fold?

No. You should call and then call again on the river. You might be losing but the situation is far less clear than previously for the following reasons:

> 1) Pre-flop, the big blind entered the pot when everyone else bar one player had folded. He does not necessarily have a very strong hand. There is a very reasonable chance that you actually have the best hand right now.

> 2) If you are behind you probably have a lot more outs. He might have a hand like J-3 or 9-3 and have flopped a lucky two pair. A sensible player would not normally play such bad hands, but in response to a late pre-flop raise many players on the big blind will call with almost anything. Against such hands you have a decent number of outs.

> 3) There are just two of you in the pot and nothing suggests that you have a strong hand. Therefore, it becomes more likely that the big blind is trying it on with nothing very much at all.

So, you call. The river brings:

The big blind bets and you call. He shows up with K♦-2♦ but he has got lucky as now your kicker fails to play and you both have the hand K-K-9-9-J and you split the pot. His call on the flop with just a king overcard was a horrible play.

Playing a Strong Draw

In previous examples we have considered play when you had a modest drawing hand and were mainly interested in whether you had sufficient pot odds to compete. Sometimes you have a much stronger drawing hand and we will now look at ways to handle such holdings.

Example 7

An early player limps and it is passed round to you on the button. You hold A♣-J♣ and you raise. Both blinds fold and the early player calls. There is $11 in the pot and two players. The flop brings:

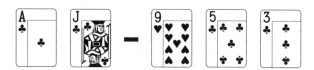

Just for a change I am going to reveal to you the hand held by the early player: he holds 10♦-9♦ and has made top pair. He is a decent, thinking player and he suspects that you might have a couple of high cards that have missed the flop (he is right), Rather than checking to the raiser and allowing you the possibility of a free card, he now bets. What do you do?

Let's look at some different ways to handle the situation:

1) Playing the Draw

You obviously have a fine drawing hand with four cards to a flush and two overcards. Thus if the early player is winning you will have up to 15 outs (nine clubs, three aces and three jacks). There is $13 in the pot and it is $2 to call. I would hope that by now you do not even need to do the pot odds calculation – it is obvious that you must easily have value for a call. Therefore you call. There is $15 in the pot and two players. The turn brings:

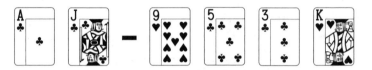

This is a rather scary card for the early player as he is worried that you have a couple of high cards and this king may have enabled you to make a pair. Nevertheless, he is a good player and if he is winning, he does not want to give a free card, so he grits his teeth and bets. He is hoping that his fear that the king has helped you is unfounded. Of course he is worried that you are playing a hand such as A-K and will now raise, putting him in an awkward situation. However, the king has not helped you but you certainly have pot odds for your draw and so you call.

Finally the river arrives:

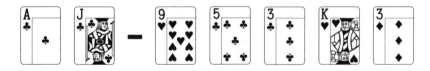

Oh dear. Your fine drawing hand has hit blanks. Your opponent again bets and you fold.

Well, that wasn't terribly successful – can we do any better?

2) The Free Card Raise

If you have gone through the earlier material carefully, I would hope that you can spot a better play on the flop. You have position and so after the early player bets out you raise. The early player is now concerned that you might have a big pocket pair and so just calls.

The turn is again the K♥ which – from the early player's point of view – is rather ugly. He checks and, as the king has not helped you, you check it back, taking your free card. As we know, unfortunately you miss your draw. However, this is at least an improvement over the previous play in that now your flop raise has saved you one small bet and, although you lose the pot, you end up $2 better off.

Nevertheless I would hope that you still find this all slightly unsatisfactory. You had a wonderful drawing hand. Couldn't you somehow have put a bit more pressure on your opponent? Indeed you could...

3) The Semi-Bluff

The semi-bluff is a powerful poker play and you must have it in your armoury. A semi-bluff is an extension of the concept of bluffing.

Everyone who has ever been exposed to poker is familiar with the idea of a bluff. In fact, if you ask some people about poker they will suggest that it is a game where the main area of skill is deciding whether your opponent is bluffing or not. Having looked through the material in this book, I would hope that by now you appreciate that poker is a rather more subtle game than this. Nevertheless, everyone knows what a bluff is. A bluff is basically a lie. You don't have a hand but you bet strongly. Your hope is that the opposition will be intimidated by your strong play and will fold. This is the only point of your play.

The semi-bluff is a more sophisticated weapon. It is a strong play made with a drawing hand. It is still basically a bluff, but now you have two ways to win:

How a semi-bluff works

1) Your opponent might believe you and fold.

2) You might complete your draw and win anyway.

On the above hand there are two ways to employ the semi-bluff: the 'normal' way and the aggressive way. Let's consider them in turn.

3a) A Normal Semi-Bluff

The flop play of the hand is identical to the play in the 'free card raise' scenario. You raise and the early player just calls. Now the K♥ comes down in the turn.

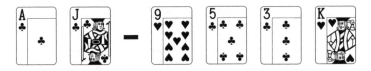

As we noted before, this is a scary card for the early player (who is holding 10♦-9♦) and he checks. In the free card scenario, you checked it back and took your free card. However, a better play is to bet.

Now the early player has a difficult decision. You have shown a great deal of strength in this hand: you raised pre-flop, you raised on the flop *and* you bet the turn. In fact, you don't actually have anything at all, but it *looks* like you must have a good hand. His bet on the flop implied that he had made a pair, but you fired straight back with a raise and then bet the turn. Surely, he will think (assuming, of course, that he thinks at all – always a dangerous assumption), you must have a big pair to play so aggressively?

At this point there is $23 in the pot and it costs him $4 to call. If you really do have a higher pair then he is playing just five outs and he does not have pot odds to call (work it out). If he thinks it through, it will be difficult for him to call here.

However, many poker players are stubborn and he may well call, suspicious that you might be bluffing and (from his point of view) having a few outs anyway. Now you have 15 outs on the river and still have a 2-to-1 chance to make the best hand anyway.

Your raise and follow up bet is a very powerful play:

1) You give him a tough decision on the turn.

2) You have a decent chance to win the hand anyway.

All in all, a classic semi-bluff.

However, there is an even more powerful way to play:

3b) An Aggressive Semi-Bluff

This time, when the early player bets the flop you simply call. Now when the K♥ arrives and he bets, you raise. You have now mimicked the play in Example 1 ('When to Raise'), when you had a big overpair and waited for the turn to pull the trigger. With a bit of luck this will scare the pants off him and he will fold. Even if he doesn't then, again, you have your 15 outs and a 2-to-1 chance to win anyway.

Which is best?

There are pros and cons to both plays. On the whole – against an average player – I would favour the line in '3a'. You put him under pressure when he has committed slightly less money to the pot, and weaker players find it easier to release hands before they get too deeply involved. Stronger players are different and against a tough player I would opt for '3b'. Tough players are less impressed with raises on the cheap street but have more respect for a raise on the expensive street. They are also more capable of giving up on a hand when they are already in deep – weaker players will usually want to see it through (often more out of curiosity than anything), whatever the cost.

 WARNING: The semi-bluff is a great play and is a powerful weapon that enables you to maximise the potential of drawing hands. However, it is more successful against better players who are capable of folding. In low-level games it should be used with caution as players in these games are often very reluctant to fold no matter how bad the situation looks.

Conditions for a successful semi-bluff

1) As few opponents as possible, preferably just one. Even two is really too many.

2) It looks as if your opponent probably has a modest holding.

3) It helps if a scare card has just appeared.

4) You have a decent number of outs if you get called.

5) Your opponent appears to be a decent player who can fold a hand.

Slowplaying

Slowplaying is a technique you can use when you have a *very* strong hand. You suspect that no-one else has very much, so if you bet then your opponents will probably just fold and you take a small pot. Instead you check to slowplay the hand and deliberately allow your opponent(s) a free card. Your hope is that now someone might pick up a little something and you can get paid off. Another way to slowplay is when somebody bets before the action gets to you. Now, rather than raising – as is justified by the strength of your hand – you just call, to encourage callers to come along behind you.

Before we go any further there is an important point to be made:

 WARNING: Slowplaying is *very* dangerous. Giving free cards is a fundamental sin in poker, and if you are going to do this on purpose you must be very sure that your hand is more or less fireproof.

If you flick back to Example 1 under the heading 'Raising on the Turn', you will see that at one point you simply called when the strength of your hand justified a raise. The point of this was to get the big raise in on the turn – the expensive street. This might feel like a slowplay but really it isn't. The point is that you were playing heads up and even if you raised (actually re-raised, but this doesn't matter – the principle is the same) on the flop, you were not going to get your opponent to fold. If a bad card was going to come there wasn't a lot you could do about it. So, you were just playing to maximise your winnings when your hand stood up.

When you make a proper slowplay you are letting players stay in the pot who would otherwise have folded and, naturally, this entails a certain risk. However, when you have a really big hand it can be a good play. Here is an example of a successful slowplay.

Example 8

You are in middle position with 8♦-8♣. An early player, who holds A♦-10♦ limps and you call. Everyone now folds round to the big blind. He holds 5♠-4♣ and he checks. There is $7 in the pot and three players. The flop comes:

The big blind has bottom pair and no kicker and so he checks. The early player has nothing at all and he also checks. You have hit a monster but if you now bet both your opponents will fold and you will pick up a tiny $7 pot, which is a bit of a shame with such a huge hand. So, you also check and the turn brings:

The big blind is now slightly irritated because he has allowed a free card. Since the flop was checked around he assumes that he was probably winning but now maybe someone has paired the ten. Nevertheless, he may still have the best hand and does not want to give a free card and so he bets. The early player has now made second pair, top kicker. It would be quite reasonable for him to raise here but he is a cautious player and he just calls. Now, of course, you raise. Your slowplay has been a big success. Both players are drawing dead and you have manipulated them into parting with extra money.

Example 9

Now we will look at a situation where slowplaying is wrong. You are in middle position with K♦-K♣. An early player limps and you raise. The button calls as do the big blind and the early player. There is $17 in the pot and four players. The flop comes:

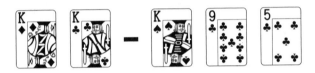

The big blind checks but the early player now bets. Is this a good place to slowplay?

Weak hold'em players assume it is. They have a huge hand and love the sensation of being able to raise on the turn and force opponents to pay two big bets. This seems like a great tactic for building the pot.

However, slowplaying in this situation can easily be disastrous and you absolutely *must* raise here. There are so many problems with just calling:

1) If you just call there will be $21 in the pot and the button and big blind can then call for $2 with nearly 11-to-1 pot odds. Now all sorts of hands have a call for value: Q-J, Q-10, J-10, 8-7, 8-6, 7-6 all have a gutshot draw.

2) Hands like 10-9, 9-8 and even 6-5 will also probably call for one bet. Although these hands cannot improve to beat you immediately, they can pick up good draws on the turn. For example, a player may now call with 10-9 and if a jack falls on the turn, then they have picked up a gutshot draw. Or someone may have A♣-5♥ and call. Now if a club comes they have

picked up the nut flush draw and again have a lot of outs. Because the pot is quite big they will undoubtedly have pot odds to pursue these draws.

This pot already stands at $19 and is likely to end up around the $35-$40 mark. By slowplaying here you are jeopardising your chances of winning the pot in order to squeeze an extra $2 or $4 out of your opponents. This is simply bad poker, as is allowing them the right price for their draws.

 TIP: A winning strategy in hold'em is to ensure that you do not allow your opponents correct pot odds to draw out against you. Whenever you do this you are effectively playing the role of the house in a casino by forcing your opponents to make bets for which they do not have the right value. They can get lucky on individual hands but – in the long run – you are making money.

If you notice the difference between the above two examples, you can see why the former is a better bet for a slowplay.

Conditions for a successful slowplay

1) The pot should be small, preferably unraised. It is almost never correct to slowplay in a raised pot.

2) The number of your opponents should also be small.

3) The board should be uncoordinated (and preferably rainbow rather than two-suited) so that it becomes less likely that your opponents will stumble into straights and flushes.

Staying out of Trouble

Quite often in hold'em you have a little something which encourages you to stay in the pot. The trouble with these 'little something' hands is that you almost certainly don't have the best hand and you can dribble away unnecessary bets by just hanging around. Sometimes your 'little something' turns into a 'medium-sized something' and this only encourages you to leak even more. If you think that you don't have the best hand (and you don't have a profitable draw) then be ruthless and dump your hand.

Example 10

An early player limps. You are in middle position with J♠-10♠ and you also limp (this is marginal – you should probably fold because there are many players still to speak and you can't guarantee the right conditions for your speculative hand). The button raises, the small blind folds, but the big blind and early player call. You also call. There is $17 in the pot and four players. The flop comes down:

The big blind checks, but the early player declines to check to the raiser and bets. There is now $19 in the pot and it is $2 to call. What do you do?

The weak, optimistic player would view the situation as follows: 'Maybe he is betting a flush draw, or even some sort of straight draw – I might actually have the best hand here with my middle pair. Even if I don't, I have five outs which is about 9-to-1 and the pot offers about 9-to-1, so I even have pot odds to play. Easy call.' And so he calls and by so doing carefully launches himself along a slippery slope.

Now watch what happens. The button (who raised pre-flop) now raises again. The big blind folds, but the early player calls. There is $27 in the pot and it is $2 to call. Now our hero begins to suspect that there isn't much chance that he has the best hand, but his pot odds are now even better (approximately 13-to-1) and so he calls. There is $29 in the pot and three players. The turn brings:

'Aaah,' he thinks. 'Two pairs – great. Good job I called.' Slightly surprisingly, the early player now bets out. There is $33 in the pot. Now our hero is a little suspicious. The board is beginning to look rather coordinated and the cards are all fairly high. He is concerned that his two-pair hand may in fact not be best. Nevertheless it might be, and even if it isn't he has approximately an 11-to-1 chance to improve to a full house on the river. His pot odds are only 8-to-1 but he reasons that his implied odds must be quite reasonable and also there is the chance that he actually has the best hand right now. He calls.

The button now raises and the early player calls. Now the pot stands at $49. Well, now there is nothing to think about. Our hero suspects that his two-pair hand is not best, but now he has clear pot odds to call for the chance to make a full house. There is $53 in the pot and the river brings:

The early player checks, as does our hero, but the button bets. The early player calls. The pot is now rather big at $61. Our hero knows he is almost certainly not winning, but calls anyway. The button has K♣-J♣ and wins. He had flopped top two pair and his hand stood up. The early player had Q♥-J♥ and had a wonderful drawing hand with flush and open-ended straight possibilities but hit a blank on the river.

Our hero's hand was completely dominated, and he had almost no chance to win the pot at any point. His innocent call on the flop ended up costing him a load of bets for which he got almost no value. Mind you, there were some good hands out against him – wasn't he a bit unlucky?

Certainly not. He just played badly. The pre-flop call is marginal but not disastrous. However, his flop call is horrible for the following reasons:

1) The button had raised pre-flop and was yet to speak. There is a great danger the pot will be raised and he will have to pay more for his feeble draw, ruining his pot odds.

2) There is a great danger that his hand is dominated. He was a bit unlucky to run into K-J, but even the early player had him dominated with his Q-J, and he only had outs to the missing tens even against him.

3) The two-flush on board is a serious concern as any 'outs' that he has to the J♥ and T♥ are tainted.

4) Both his opponents were clearly interested in this pot, so there is always going to be the danger of raises and re-raises. Our hero is sandwiched and in such circumstances you can end up paying through the nose for your draw.

River Play

When you get to see the river card no further improvement to your hand is possible. The river is a tense moment. Sometimes you have had the best hand all along but maybe one or more opponents have been playing drawing hands against you. You are naturally concerned that their drawing hands might have got there and your hand may no longer be best.

Some players are capable of taking the initiative and playing hands very aggressively on the flop and turn but then freeze up when the river comes. Some vaguely scary card lands on the board and they are worried that if they bet, they will get raised and then feel obliged to call. Not only will they suffer the pain of losing a big pot but they will have tossed away an extra bet on the river to boot. So they freeze. They check and their opponent checks the hand back. It turns out they were winning but their opponent had a good enough hand to call. By freezing up, they have thrown away a bet.

Mind you, they probably won't care, or even realise that they have made a mistake. They will just be happy that their hand has stood up and they have taken down the pot. This is a bad attitude.

 TIP: A major element of the skill in limit hold'em is about squeezing the maximum possible profit from your winning hands. Failing to pick up easy bets on the river is a bad error.

Occasionally, it is fairly obvious that your hand may no longer be good and a check is in order. However, whenever you have position over your opponent and they have already checked then you should almost always bet. If they really had made a good hand they might well have bet, being concerned that you might simply check behind them.

It takes experience to be able to judge these situations well, but here are some examples.

Example 11

You are on the button with J♠-J♦. A middle players opens with a raise and you re-raise. Everyone folds and the middle player calls. You see the flop heads up and it arrives:

This is a very good flop – no overcards. Your opponent checks, you bet and he calls. The turn is a blank – the 4♠ and again the play goes check, bet and he calls. The river is the K♠ and your opponent checks.

Now the weak player thinks: 'Oh dear. An overcard. Maybe he

has A-K or even K-Q and has outdrawn by making a pair. I'd better play safe and check.' So he checks, his opponent shows 9♠-9♣ and our safety-first expert has thrown away a bet.

Checking the river here is way too feeble. Sure, he might have a king but:

1) There are a load of other hands he might be calling with, e.g. A-Q, A-J, Q-10, J-10, 10-9 or any smallish pair etc. Some players, especially at the low limits will call you down with any old rubbish.

2) If he really did have a king he might well have bet the river himself.

 WARNING: An important part of poker is trying to read your opponents' hands and decide what sort of cards they might be playing. This is *not* the same as forever fearing the worst and assuming that any remotely scary card that arrives is bound to help them. Poker is not a game for pessimists.

Basic principle for betting the river

If, on the balance of probabilities, you are winning, *and* you can get called by a worse hand, then bet.

This principle certainly applied in Example 11. Here is another example.

Example 12

A middle player limps and you raise from the button with A♠-10♠. The blinds fold and the middle player calls. You see the flop heads up and it comes down:

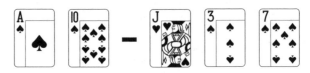

Your opponent now bets. You have a fine draw with a four-flush and an overcard and make the good play of raising. The middle player calls. The turn is the 2♦, he checks and now you prefer to bet rather than take the free card. He calls. This is the situation:

Now if the river is a complete blank and your opponent checks, you should check behind him and hope that your hand is good. It probably isn't, but if he can beat ace high he will certainly call, so betting accomplishes nothing. However, If the river is the 10♦, then you should bet. It is quite possible that he has a hand such as 8-8, 9-9, an even smaller pair, or that he has a hand with a seven. He will probably call with all of these. It is possible that he has a jack, but with top pair in a heads-up situation he may well have played more aggressively than he actually did. A bet here should have positive expectation, which is the key factor. Thus, if on three occasions he calls and you win, whilst on one occasion he calls and turns up with a jack, then you have made money with the bet.

Putting it all Together

Finally, let's play through a hand featuring four strong, thinking players. We will go through their thought processes and see how they employ a number of the strategems outlined earlier in this chapter. Note how these players try to think not only about what they personally are trying to achieve in the hand but also about what they other players are doing. Trying to get inside your opponents' heads is a hallmark of a strong poker player.

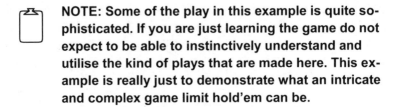 **NOTE:** Some of the play in this example is quite sophisticated. If you are just learning the game do not expect to be able to instinctively understand and utilise the kind of plays that are made here. This example is really just to demonstrate what an intricate and complex game limit hold'em can be.

Example 13

This hand is from a $20-$40 game and features four key players: Billy is in the big blind, Charlie is an early player, Dennis is a middle position player and Harry is on the button.

They hold the following hands:

Billy: 8♦-6♦
Charlie: 9♥-9♠
Dennis: 6♣-6♠
Harry: Q♣-J♣

Charlie is first to speak. He has a good hand with his pair of nines, but is UTG and is reluctant to open with a raise. With nine players still to speak there is a danger someone may have a higher pair and re-raise, when Charlie will end up heads up with a dominated hand. Charlie therefore elects to call.

Implied Odds

Dennis is in middle position with his pair of sixes. He can see that Charlie is already in the pot and suspects that if he calls, one or two other players may also call. If the blinds then play, the flop will be taken five- or six-handed and he will have good implied odds to flop a set. Nevertheless, this call is slightly loose play. There may well be a raise behind him and this will dissuade other players from entering the pot and reduce Charlie's pot odds as well as obliging him to pay extra to see the flop. If there were already two (or even better, three) players who had limped then this call is fine. As it is, it is slightly better to fold.

Position

Harry is on the button with Q♣-J♣. This is a decent hand and he has the best position at the table. He can certainly call, but Harry decides to raise which, in these particular circumstances, is a good play, for the following reasons:

> 1) Charlie and Dennis only limped in rather than raising, so they probably don't have very strong hands. Therefore it is not that likely that Harry's hand is dominated. Anyone with a hand as strong as A-Q or A-J would probably have raised.
>
> 2) Thus, if the flop arrives queen high or jack high, Harry may well have the best hand.
>
> 3) With suited connectors he also has a good drawing hand and may get lucky with flush and straight possibilities. Having prime position will also allow him to exploit these possibilities to the full as he may be able to make a free card play.

The fact that Harry can make a good raise with his quite modest hand demonstrates how important position is. Being on the button allows you to control the play to a certain extent and Harry is utilising his position to the full.

Implied Odds

The small blind folds and Billy is in the big blind with 8♦-6♦ – a low-ish, suited one-gapper. This is not much of a hand but he anticipates that there will be four players seeing the flop and he is getting 7-to-1 pot odds for a call (Harry's raise brings the bet to $40, but Billy has already put up $20 as the big blind). Billy decides to call, which is a borderline decision. Folding is probably slightly better as his hand really is quite weak.

Charlie and Dennis both call. There are four players in, the pot is $170 and the flop comes down:

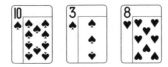

Avoiding Trouble

Billy has middle pair with a bad kicker. This is one those classic 'little something' hands that were discussed earlier. However, it is not out of the question that he is currently in the lead and, if he is, he should bet out to protect his hand. However, upon consideration of the situation he prefers to check. There are various factors affecting this decision:

1) If anyone has an eight, a ten or a high pair, he is behind with not many outs. With three opponents this is more likely than not.

2) If he does bet, it is quite likely that someone will raise. If this happens he will end up putting $40 into a pot which will be approximately $200. His hand is a five-outer (assuming his outs are good) and this represents insufficient pot odds.

3) He is stuck with bad position for the whole hand.

4) The pot has been raised and so you expect players' hands to be better than if it was an unraised pot.

Billy is well aware of the danger of dribbling away bets with a fairly feeble holding and his decision to check is very sensible. This is further confirmation of the principle that when you are playing a speculative hand you are – in general – looking to make more than a pair.

Avoiding a Free Card

The action now passes to Charlie with his 9♥-9♠. Charlie is moderately pleased with the flop. Harry has raised pre-flop and there is a decent chance that Harry made this play with two random high cards, say A-K or A-Q or maybe something even slightly weaker. Charlie is only in trouble if someone has a ten and it is not that likely that Harry has a ten. Of course, there is a danger is that Harry has a big pair, but you cannot always assume that your opponents have their best possible hands.

Charlie is concerned that if he checks and then Dennis and Harry both check there are a great number of bad cards that can come on the turn that will mess up his chances. Any overcard or any spade will obviously be bad. He therefore decides to bet to avoid the danger of giving a free card.

Avoiding Trouble

Dennis is next to speak and is looking at a pair of sixes. Now that the flop has come down this does not look like much of a hand. There are two overcards and if he is behind – which is more likely than not – then he is playing just two outs. Of course, Charlie might be betting a drawing hand with, for example, two spades, J-9 or 9-7. However, if he decides to call there is a danger of further action behind him; Harry and Billy can still raise. He folds and this is an easy decision.

Semi-Bluff/Free Card Raise

Next to speak is Harry and he likes the look of the flop. He has two overcards and a gutshot draw. So, if he is behind against Charlie then he has up to ten outs (Charlie may have a hand like J-10 or Q-10 which will reduce his outs to seven but, even if this is the case, this is still a decent number). Harry is certainly going to play the hand and recognises quickly that this is an excellent moment for a raise. He does not even have to decide how he will continue on the turn. Assuming that Billy folds and Charlie just calls then he can either pursue his semi-bluff with a further bet (he should certainly do this if a scare card such as an ace arrives) or he can take a free card.

Essentially, Harry wants to take control of the pot and raising gives him the chance to do this.

Billy now has an easy decision. He didn't think his feeble hand was worth playing even when no-one had bet. Now that there has been a bet and a raise he is certain that his hand is worthless and he folds.

Controlled Aggression/Avoiding the Free Card

Play now comes back to Charlie. There is currently $230 in the pot and he is facing Harry's raise. It will cost him $20 to call.

Charlie is not that intimidated by Harry's raise. Charlie is a good player and he knows that it is quite likely that Harry is trying for a free card on the turn. The danger still exists that Harry has an overpair, but there is also a very good chance that Charlie's hand is best right now. Charlie realises this and he wants to make sure that if this is indeed the case, then Harry is paying as much as possible to try and draw him out. If Charlie is not going to passively fall in with Harry's plans (i.e. call the raise and then check the turn), then he has two options:

The strong, solid play

Charlie can call the raise and wait to see the turn card. If the turn card is a safe one (i.e. not a spade and not an overcard), then he will bet out again, preventing Harry from getting his free card.

The strong, aggressive play

Charlie can re-raise on the flop and, assuming Harry calls, then bet out on the turn.

I would say either of these methods is fine and both are preferable to the rather feeble call/check strategy. Charlie is a strong, aggressive player and he decides he is going to send a message to Harry. He re-raises.

Harry is slightly taken aback. He did not expect Charlie to play back at him like this and now he is not sure how strong Charlie's hand is. He may be very strong. Nevertheless there is now $270 in the pot and, even if his only out is to the gutshot (for example, if Charlie has a set), he still has pot odds to play. He calls. There is $290 in the pot and the turn brings:

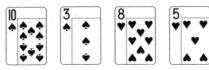

Charlie is pleased to see this card. It is not an overcard and also it is not a spade. He now bets.

Adjusting the Pot Odds

There is now $330 in the pot and it is $40 to Harry, who now considers the situation. Charlie is sending him a message that he has a good hand but Harry also knows that Charlie is capable of pushing hard without necessarily having a monster. Harry knows that he has an absolute minimum of four outs (unless Charlie has the precise – and highly unlikely – holding of 8♠-5♠) and could have as many as ten. In the circumstances, Harry decides his hand is worth a total of about seven or eight outs. The pot odds are around 8-to-1 and so, even with six outs, Harry has a reasonable call. Seven or eight make the call easy and so Harry calls. There is $370 in the pot and the river brings:

Inducing a Bluff

It is again Charlie's turn to speak. Let's now see how different players will consider the situation.

The weak player

The weak player thinks to himself, 'Phew, I got to the river safely and there haven't been any overcards on the turn or river. This pot is quite big enough already. Let's just check and see who has the best hand.'

The stronger player

The stronger player thinks, 'Good, no unpleasant overcards. I suspect I have the best hand now. I mustn't let extra river bets slip through my fingers. I will bet the hand and try to pick up an extra big bet.'

The very strong player

The very strong player looks deeper into the position and reasons as follows, 'I re-raised him on the flop and he just called. I then bet the turn and again, he just called. It rather looks as if he has some sort of drawing hand and he was indeed making a semi-bluff play with his flop raise, but backed off when I played back at him.'

He then continues, 'If he has a drawing hand (with a couple of spades or a couple of high cards) then he has missed and now has no hand at all. If I bet he will just fold, but what if I check? Then it might look like it has been me who has been pushing the draw and that now I have missed. In these circumstances he might bet the river as a final bluff which I can then pick of with a call.'

Charlie is a very strong player (or maybe he is not that good, but he is having a good day), reasons this all out and checks. This play is *inducing a bluff*.

The Bluff

Harry is disappointed that he has missed his draw but is surprised at Charlie's check. He is staring down at queen high and now realises that, even if Charlie has been running a semi-bluff with a spade draw, he might still be losing to a hand like K♠-J♠ or A♠-9♠. However, if he now bets, Charlie might well fold such hands. and he will have stolen the pot.

There is $370 in the pot and he can bet for just $40. It looks too good an opportunity to pass by and so ... he falls right into Charlie's trap and bets. Charlie, of course, calls and takes down a nice pot.

Charlie's classy play on the river has yielded him an extra big bet. Had Charlie bet the river Harry would, of course, have folded.

But what if Harry had a really Big Hand?

This has been a very interesting hand with both players trying to out-think each other. However, I can imagine that some readers might be rather sceptical of Charlie's outright aggression in this pot when he had a pair lower than one of the board cards, was playing out of position and his opponent had shown such strength both pre-flop and on the flop. 'If I tried that,' they might be thinking, 'I would surely have run into an opponent holding A-A and would have just lost myself even more money with all this aggression.'

This is a fair point. So let's rewind to the flop play to just after Charlie had re-raised. The board is as follows:

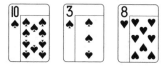

As we know Charlie is holding 9♥-9♠ and has just re-raised. The pot stands at $270. Harry, of course, has Q♣-J♣ and decides to just call. However, let's allow him to exchange his hand for a biggie: A♣-A♥. Now what will he do?

He will probably cap the pot. He will not believe that he is losing this hand. Charlie would need to have a very convenient hand such as a set or 10-8 for this to be the case. He will probably think that Charlie has a very good draw and will want to make him pay the maximum to pursue it. So he caps the pot and Charlie calls. Now the turn brings:

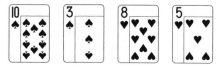

Charlie now checks and Harry bets. Charlie gets the message and folds. 'What was the point of that?' you may well ask, 'Didn't he just throw away a load of money with a hopeless hand?'

No, he didn't. His play actually *saved* money. Let's see why this is the case. When Harry initially raises on the flop Charlie can just call, instead of re-raising as he did. As we know, he suspects that Harry just has a draw. Therefore he is suspicious enough to call him down, assuming that blanks arrive on the turn and river.

So, Charlie calls the raise. Thus the flop round costs him $40. Then the blank arrives on the turn, he checks, Harry bets and he calls. This costs him another $40. Finally the same thing happens on the river and he ends up paying yet another $40. Total bill for seeing the hand through: $40 + $40 + $40 = $120.

What happened instead? Charlie re-raised and Harry capped the pot. Thus the flop ended up costing Charlie a whopping $80. However, he gained the crucial information that Harry had a seriously big hand, realised he was playing just two outs, and folded. Total bill: $80. This is a $40 saving over the check/call method.

Is there any problem with all this? Yes, there is. Harry could be bluffing and you might have put a load of money into the pot only to throw away the winning hand. Is this likely? No. It is extremely unlikely. Look at Harry's play: he has raised pre-flop, raised on the flop, capped the betting on the flop and then bet the turn. In the meantime you have suggested that you have a pretty decent hand yourself, but he just doesn't care and has responded by making four consecutive aggressive plays. Believe me – he has a big hand and your pair of nines is not best.

The Benefits of Aggression

This example demonstrates why aggressive play is so important. When you are ahead in the pot you force your opponents to pay the maximum to chase their draws. When you show a lot of strength and yet they still play back at you, this gives you vital information about where you stand and you end up paying less with your losing hands.

 TIP: Playing aggressively intimidates your opponents and forces them onto the back foot. If they know that any time they bet you are likely to raise and that any time they raise you are likely to re-raise then this will inhibit their play. If they are easily cowed you will force them into check/call mode which is exactly where you want them.

Don't try this at Home

To be able to play like this requires a great deal of good judgment which generally only comes through the experience of playing a lot of hold'em. Do not try and play like this when you start out. If you do, you really will end up throwing money at pots where you are a big underdog.

If you start out your hold'em career playing in $0.50-$1 or $1-$2 games it is most unlikely that your opponents will show this kind of sophistication in their play. Concentrate on playing a sensible, solid game and you will do well.

Chapter Eleven

Final Thoughts

- ♣ Caveat Emptor
- ♣ What to do Next
- ♣ Further Reading
- ♣ Results and Running Bad
- ♣ Keeping Track

With any luck the material in this book will have demonstrated what an intricate and exciting game limit hold'em can be, and you are now itching to play live poker or sign up with an online cardroom, start playing and put into practice what you have learnt. Before you do so, there are a few practical considerations.

Caveat Emptor

When I was at school one of the subjects I studied up to what was then known as 'O' level (Ordinary Level) was physics. The course work was all very interesting and I therefore decided that I would pursue physics and signed up for the 'A' level (Advanced Level) course. On the first day of the 'A' level course our teacher informed us that: 'That stuff you learnt for 'O' level is all rubbish. You can forget all that; now we will teach you what really happens.'

Of course the 'O' level course was not *exactly* complete rubbish. What he meant was that the way that concepts such as light, gravity and the structure of atoms had been dealt with was – necessarily – rather simplified and in some cases, over-simplified. There is an element of this in how I feel about some of the strategy recommendations made in this book.

In many ways poker is a difficult game to study. With a game like chess a good move is a good move – end of story. Whether you are a world champion or a beginner it doesn't matter. If a move leads to checkmate, then it's a good move and it will win the game for you. Poker is more slippery. Good 'moves' against weaker players are just not the same as good moves against stronger players. Poker is very situational and it is not just a case of whether an opponent is strong or weak. Sometimes the key factor deciding how you should approach a situation depends upon another characteristic of their play, such as whether they are passive or aggressive, or whether they are loose or tight.

I am sure that all the suggestions I have made in this book are fine for players starting out in the game of limit hold'em and playing at the low limits (which I would define as anything up to $3-$6). In fact I would go further. I would suggest that if you understand all the material in this book and are capable of putting it into practice then you can play at the low limits without being an underdog in the game. Simply playing the right starting hands, in the right positions and for the right reasons, will give you an edge over maybe 80% of the players in those games.

However, if you get into hold'em and find that you can compete successfully at the low limits then at some point you will probably want to move up and maybe try $5-$10 or even higher. Now, in general, the play gets tougher and if you want to prosper, you will need a better understanding of the game and more sophistication in your play. However, this is not a problem. There are plenty of other books which are aimed at players who are trying to move beyond a basic game and I have recommended a number of these in the 'Further Reading' section.

What to do Next

If you want to get involved in poker then sign up with an online cardroom and join the games at a low limit that you can afford. Even if you are very wealthy and can afford to lose thousands of dollars there is still little point trying to start your hold'em career by playing $20-$40. The likelihood is that you will get crushed and you will have no idea why. Even if you can cope with the potential financial hit, the experience will simply be frustrating. The probable outcome is that you will just lose and will be none the wiser as to why this has happened.

As a beginning player you need to get a good few months practice at levels where the play is not so tough so that you develop the all-important *feel* for how limit hold'em works. Once you feel comfortable at this level, you can try moving up. If you feel comfortable at this new level, then all well and good. If, however, you feel out of your depth (incidentally this will demonstrate an excellent sense of self-awareness which is a pretty useful trait to have as a poker player) then be prepared to drop back down again.

Further Reading

Once you feel you have mastered the material in this book and can put it into practice consistently you will want to look a little deeper into the game, especially if you are thinking about moving up in limits. The following are all good books and, generally, deal with more advanced concepts.

 WARNING: There is very little point reading any of these books if you are a beginner. They deal with some quite difficult concepts and you need to have a decent amount of hold'em experience before they will make much sense to you. If you try to absorb these concepts as a beginner you will be trying to run before you can walk.

Hold'em Poker for Advanced Players (21st Century Edition), Sklansky and Malmuth (Two Plus Two Publishing)
This is the classic treatise on hold'em, written by the two most respected authors on the game.

Small Stakes Hold'em: Winning Big with Expert Play, Miller, Sklansky and Malmuth (Two Plus Two Publishing)
This is billed as the way to maximise your potential in the low-limit games. Indeed it is, but much of the advice can also be applied to hold'em played at any level.

Middle Limit Hold'em Poker, Ciaffone and Brier (Bob Ciaffone)
This is based around several hundred puzzles which discuss play in almost all situations that can arise in hold'em.

Internet Texas Hold'em, Hilger (www.internettexasholdem.com)
Weighing the Odds in Hold'em Poker, King Yao (Pi Yee Press)

Both these books offer much useful insight into how to deal with more advanced concepts at limit hold'em.

How Good is Your Limit Hold'em?, Jacobs and Brier (D & B Publishing)

This book concentrates on how to adapt your play by focusing on the different styles of your opponents.

Results and Running Bad

If you can meet with triumph and disaster,
And treat those two imposters just the same
If – Rudyard Kipling

All poker players suffer the unhappy experience of *running bad*. It happens to beginners, good players, bad players and world champions. Running bad is when the cards just do not fall for you. You seem completely unable to hit any of your draws; when you do get your big hands some bozo is forever hitting a ridiculous card to beat you on the river, and when you get dealt K-K, someone else has A-A. When this happens for long enough (and believe me it can happen for a *very* long time), it inevitably starts to play tricks with your mind. Running bad can happen not just for hours or days or even weeks, but sometimes for months.

The luck factor in poker is considerable. If you sit down one evening in a $2-$4 game, play well over a 250-hand session and win $120, then that's wonderful and I am very happy for you. However, please do not suddenly think that you are a wonderful player and you can crush this game forever. This is not necessarily the case. The result of a 250-hand session is *nothing* for judging your skill at a certain level. You may be surprised by this but even one hundred times this amount, e.g. 25,000 hands is not really enough.

The following statistic is rather sobering. Over an 18-month period up to the beginning of 2005, I played exclusively in moderately high-level games on one particular site. Overall it was a successful experience and I won approximately 2,000 big bets.

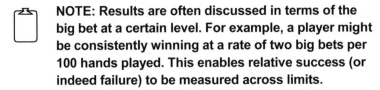 **NOTE: Results are often discussed in terms of the big bet at a certain level. For example, a player might be consistently winning at a rate of two big bets per 100 hands played. This enables relative success (or indeed failure) to be measured across limits.**

I played fairly consistently in terms of time played per month and my average win was – obviously – just over 100 big bets per month. Do you think I won every month I played? No. Not even close. I had 14 winning months but four losing ones as well. In fact, one month I even lost 250 big bets. I also experienced a five-month spell where I recorded a small loss. This is quite remarkable. Playing in a game where – in the long run – I had a fairly clear edge, I experienced a barren spell of five months, probably representing around 300 hours play.

Tilt

A typical effect of running bad is that players go on tilt. Tilt is when an adverse run of cards affects your play and causes you to make bad decisions. Typically, you experience two or three horrible drawouts and find yourself well down on a session. Then, either in an attempt to recoup your losses or maybe simply out of pure frustration, you begin to play moderate hands far too aggressively. Obviously, you are just playing bad poker and the most likely outcome is that you will lose even more money.

I suspect that every poker player in the world experiences tilt to some degree or other. When you are having a horrible session and some clown rivers a fifth consecutive gutshot against you, it's very hard indeed to control your emotions and maintain your 'A' game. Everyone has to find their own way to deal with it. My own personal approach involves a waste paper bin which is by the side of my desk. When I sense myself beginning to tilt I take out my frustration on the bin, usually by kicking it. This bin now sports a rather sad collection of dents as a testimony to all the bad beats I have taken over the years.

There is also another more subtle form of tilt which can affect your play. You know full well that you need to play your good hands hard but when you keep getting drawn out anyway, you can slip into a defeatist mentality. You think, 'I've got a good hand, but what's the point of raising? Either there will be a monster hand out against me or someone will draw out anyway.' You then slip into negative, passive play which, in its own way, is just as bad as wild, aggressive play – possibly even worse.

There is no simple solution to any of this. However, it helps to keep the following in mind:

 NOTE: If you are a good player and you play better than your opponents, they will appear to be much luckier than you.

If you play well, then the majority of the time that a big pot develops you should have the best of it. It should be you holding the big hand and your opponents trying to draw you out. This will happen reasonably frequently and it will *feel* like you are being unlucky. However, much of the time it won't happen and overall you will show a healthy profit from these encounters.

Meanwhile, much less often, it will be you who is taking the worst of it. Then, occasionally, you will have a lucky drawout that goes in your favour. However, you will do this to your opponents much less often than they will do it to you. The reason is that to benefit from a lucky drawout, you have to have the worst of it in the first place. If you are a good player this is a situation that you want for your opponents and not for you.

Finally, if you find yourself struggling in a horrible session then it might help to bear the following in mind.

 TIP: In a roundabout way, you can still make money when you get terrible cards and no luck. Just ensure that you keep your cool and lose the absolute minimum – even if that turns out to be quite a big hit. One day, your opponents will get these same terrible cards and, if they lack your self-control, they will lose even more. When that happens *you* will be the beneficiary.

Keeping Track

Keeping track of your results is very important, even if you are only a casual player. This does not need to be terribly sophisticated. Just keep a diary (or preferably a spreadsheet), noting the date, the game you played, number of hours (or hands – or both if statistics really fascinate you) and your result. If you are going to succeed as a poker player you need to be ruthlessly honest about your abilities. It is no good believing that you are 'about a break-even player' if your credit card indicates that you are haemorrhaging $2,000 every month. Keeping track of results will keep you honest with yourself.

Self Analysis

A big problem with poker is that an increase in skill is not necessarily reflected by an immediate improvement in results. If you take some tennis coaching and improve your game you will probably find that you can now beat opponents who previously beat you. Furthermore if you are better than them, you will probably beat them 90% of the time. Not so in poker. As we already know, you can play much better than your opponents and suffer the galling experience of watching them beat you time and time again.

It is therefore good practice to go over a session and perform a post mortem, especially if it was a losing session. Did you play all the hands okay and were you just unlucky with a few random cards or did you get sucked in too often without a good enough hand?

 TIP: The important thing in poker is not to win money but to play well. If you play well for long enough, the money will take care of itself.

There are a number of commercial software packages which can help with this. My own favourite is PokerTracker (www.pokertracker.com) but there are others. If you play your poker on one of the major sites then you will usually find that the hand histories log automatically to your hard disk. You can feed these into PokerTracker (or whatever you choose) and it will tell you all sorts of fascinating things about your play and that of your opponents. As well as being an excellent record of your play, this is also an invaluable aid to analysis. Even if you just play a little poker as a hobby, I would strongly recommend that you acquire one of these packages. Anyone who plays poker seriously without one is simply handicapping themselves.

Solutions to Exercises

Exercise One

1) A straight: the sequence Q-J-10-9-8.

2) Two pair: a pair of queens and a pair of sevens.

3) Three of a kind: three nines.

4) A flush: all the cards are spades.

5) Nine high: there are no straights, flushes or pairs.

6) A straight: the sequence 5-4-3-2-A.

7) A full house: three tens and two fours.

8) A pair: two kings.

9) Four of a kind: four fives.

10) A straight flush: the sequence 10-9-8-7-6 and all the cards are hearts.

11) Two pair: two aces and two kings.

12) Jack high: no pairs, straights or flushes.

13) A full house: three twos and two fives.

14) A flush: all the cards are hearts.

15) A straight: the sequence A-K-Q-J-10.

Exercise Two

1) 'a' wins: a flush beats a straight.

2) 'a' wins: a full house beats a flush.

3) 'b' wins: a straight beats three of a kind.

4) 'a' wins: three of a kind beats two pair.

5) 'b' wins: two pair beats one pair.

6) 'b' wins: one pair beats a high card.

7) 'a' wins: full house tens beats a full house twos.

8) 'b' wins: two straights but the A-K-Q-J-10 beats the 5-4-3-2-A.

9) 'a' wins: two flushes but A-10-9 beats A-10-8.

10) 'b' wins: a straight flush beats a flush.

11) 'a' wins: two pairs aces and threes beats two pairs kings and queens.

12) 'a' wins: a straight flush beats a straight.

13) 'b' wins: three of a kind threes beats three of a kind twos.

14) 'b' wins: ace high beats king high.

15) 'a' wins: both sides have two pairs, jacks and tens, but the nine kicker beats the eight kicker.

16) 'b' wins: both sides have a pair of aces but the Q-J beats the Q-9.

17) 'b' wins: both sides have three of a kind sevens but the A-Q beats the A-9.

18) 'b' wins: a pair of nines beats a pair of eights.

19) a tie: the two sides have identical flushes.

Exercise Three

1) Three of a kind: jacks.

2) A straight: 8-7-6-5-4.

3) A flush in spades.

4) One pair: a pair of fours.

5) Two pairs: kings and tens. The pair of fives is irrelevant.

6) A full house: nines full of sevens.

7) Four of a kind: eights.

8) A straight flush: Q-J-10-9-8 of hearts.

9) A straight: 9-8-7-6-5 (note this is better than 8-7-6-5-4).

10) A flush in diamonds.

Exercise Four

1) You have a straight (J-10-9-8-7). This is the nut hand. No-one can have a stronger hand than this.

2) You have a straight (K-Q-J-10-9). However, with three hearts on the board anyone with two hearts will have a flush which will beat you.

3) You have the top straight (A-K-Q-J-10). However, the pair on board means that someone can have a full house or possibly even quad sevens. There are many ways for players to have a full house here: A-A, Q-Q, J-J, A-7, Q-7 and J-7 all generate a full house.

4) You have a straight (J-10-9-8-7). There are no pairs on the board and no flush possibilities, so you might think you have the nut hand. However, you don't. Anyone with Q-J has a higher straight (Q-J-10-9-8). This is another example of the weakness of hands that rely on one card. It's not that likely that someone has Q-J, but it can happen.

5) You have a flush with your two diamonds matching up with the three on the board. However, you have only the second nut flush. Anyone with A-x in diamonds will beat you.

6) You have a set of tens which is the second nuts. There are no straight or flush possibilities, but you will lose if someone has K-K for a higher set.

7) You have a full house and it is the nut hand. No-one can have Q-Q for quads because there are insufficient queens left in the deck. Other players can have full houses, but they will all be weaker than yours.

8) You again have a big full house (in fact the nut full house) but there are two hands that beat you. A player with 7-7 has quad sevens, while a player with 10♠-9♠ has made a straight flush.

9) Any spade will give you a flush, while any eight or three will

generate a straight (allying with the existing 7-6-5-4 sequence). However, any spade or heart creates the possibility of a flush for an opponent. Therefore you have precisely four cards to the nuts: 3♦, 3♣, 8♦, 8♣.

10) You have the sequence 9-8-7-6 so any ten or five will generate a straight. Since the board features one card of each suit, there is no chance for anyone to make a flush. However – be careful. A ten will also lead to the board having the combination A-J-10. Anyone with K-Q will then have a higher straight.

Exercise Five

1) The small blind in a $10-$20 game is $5.

2) The big blind in a $3-$6 game is $3.

3) The small blind is on the dealer's immediate left.

4) The big blind is last to speak on the pre-flop betting round.

5) In a $1-$2 game the betting unit on the flop round is $1.

6) In a $50-$100 game the betting unit on the turn round is $100.

7) $30. The initial raise brings the bet to $20. In order to raise again you must put in a further $10.

8) The small blind is first to speak on all rounds except the pre-flop round.

9) In a $10-$20 game the small blind has already put up $5 and must thus put a further $5 in to call.

10) A round of betting consists of a maximum of one bet and three raises.

Exercise Six

1) Andrew is winning with a pair of kings against a pair of jacks. Barry has just two outs: the two remaining jacks. Pairing his queen will not help him – his queens and jacks will lose to Andrew's kings and fours.

2) Andrew is winning with a pair of nines against Ace high.

Barry has ten outs: three aces and three queens will give him a higher pair, while now four jacks will complete a straight (A-K-Q-J-10).

3) Barry is winning with a pair of jacks against a pair of nines. Here we have a strange situation where if either player improves to three of a kind then the other automatically completes a straight (K-Q-J-10-9). A nine will make a straight for Barry while a jack will make a straight for Andrew. Andrew has just two outs – the two missing jacks.

4) Andrew is winning with three of a kind against a pair of tens. Barry has eight outs: four jacks and four sixes, any of which will complete his straight. Note that tens and nines are of no help as Andrew's set of kings is such a strong hand.

5) Barry is currently ahead with a pair of jacks against just ace high. This hand is complicated so let's consider each high card in turn.

a) Aces. These give Andrew a pair of aces which are good enough to overtake Barry's lower pair. Three outs.

b) Kings. These complete a straight for Andrew (A-K-Q-J-10). Four outs.

c) Queens. These give Andrew a pair of queens, *but* they will also complete a straight for Barry (Q-J-10-9-8). They are not outs.

d) Jacks. These don't help Andrew. Zero outs.

e) Tens. Again, no help. Zero outs.

f) Nines. This time it is Andrew who completes the Q-J-10-9-8 straight. Three outs.

Nothing else helps Andrew, so he has a total of ten outs.

6) Barry is winning with a pair of aces against a pair of nines. Andrew has nine outs: three jacks and four sixes will give him a straight, and two nines will give him three of a kind. Andrew's other outs – the three sevens to make two pair – are tainted. Any sevens on the board will give Barry a straight (J-10-9-8-7).

7) Barry is winning with a flush against Andrew's pair of

kings. Andrew has six outs: his A♥ means that any of the remaining hearts will give him a bigger flush on the river, *except*
the J♥ which will complete a straight flush for Barry.

8) Andrew is winning with a flush against two pair. Barry has
four outs: the two aces and two queens will give a full house.

9) Barry is winning with two pair, nines and threes against
just a pair of nines. Andrew has 16 outs – a surprising total.
They are made up as follows: ten outs arise with 'normal' three
kings, three queens and four tens (straight: K-Q-J-10-9), but
the three fours and three jacks also win for Andrew as these
render Barry's pair of threes worthless. Both players will then
have two pair, nines and jacks (or fours), but Andrew's king
kicker will be decisive.

10) Barry is winning with a full house against Andrew's three
of a kind. Andrew has seven outs: three aces and three jacks
improve him to a better full house, while the easy-to-overlook
6♣ puts four of a kind on board, obliterates Barry's pair of fives
and enables Andrew to win with his ace kicker.

Exercise Seven

1) There are 13 hearts and 39 non-hearts. The chances are
39-to-13 which is 3-to-1.

2) There are 2 black aces and 50 other cards. The chances are
50-to-2 which is 25-to-1.

3) You can win with three aces, three kings (bigger pair) and
four queens (straight) – a total of ten outs. There are 44 outstanding cards (52 less the eight shared between your two
hands and the board). Thus your chances are 34-to-10. This is
approximately 3½-to-1 which can also be expressed as 7-to-2.

4) You can win with two nines (trips), four eights (straight) and
three sevens (two pair) – a total of nine outs. There are 44 outstanding cards. Thus your chances are 35-to-9 which is approximately 4-to-1.

5) You can win with two nines (trips) and three eights (two
pair) – a total of five outs. Again there are 44 outstanding

cards so your odds are thus 39-to-5, or about 8-to-1. The pot odds are 10-to-1 and so you should call.

6) Now you can only win with two nines (trips) for a total of two outs. The eights will make you a two-pair hand, but the pair of fours on the board means that your opponent will have a stronger two-pair hand with aces up. There are 44 outstanding cards so your odds are thus 42-to-2, or 21-to-1. The pot odds are 10-to-1 and so you should fold.

Exercise Eight

1) If you are going to play any of these hands you should raise to maximise the chances of winning at once. The hands worth playing – and thus raising with – are 'a', 'b' and 'c'. The other three should be folded. The pair of threes is too weak a pair; A♥-7♦ is not much better than playing a bare ace, and 9♣-8♣ is just a reasonable drawing hand and is not playable when you have no idea how the pot will develop.

2a) You almost certainly have the best hand and you have prime position – you must raise.

2b) Another excellent holding – again a raise is called for.

2c) This is a clear call. The pot will probably be taken at least five-handed – you have excellent implied odds to flop a set. There is no reason to raise.

2d) You can also call here. This is a speculative hand of course, but it will play well in a multi-way pot. It is suited, connected and you have excellent position.

2e) Calling here is also fine. You are hoping for a flush draw but no-one has shown any strength so you may have the best hand if an ace flops.

2f) Fold. When there are many limpers in pre-flop you can speculate with a lot of drawing hands. This one, however, just does not have enough going for it. There is little high card strength, it is offsuit and it is a two-gapper. Dump it.

3a) Call. This is fine for a call. It is possible you have the best hand, but with three players in for two bets you are probably in trouble with any overcard. Also you have bad position so raising here is over-aggressive (it will be unpleasant if you raise and another player then caps). It is fine to call and see what kind if flop you get.

3b) Call. You can also call here even though the hand is rather weak and you are quite likely to be dominated by a higher pair. There are already 7½ small bets in the pot and it costs you just 1½ bets to call. This means you have pot odds of 5-to-1 (also, the big blind may very well call and this makes your pot odds even better). Now if you can hit your set you will be in very good shape to win a large pot.

3c) Call. This is good enough to call. A-K is a very clear call and A-J would be borderline. A-10 you should fold. You have bad position and you will need to connect with the flop, but A-Q should certainly be played here.

3d) Fold. This is a nice hand, but it is just too weak to play out of position for 1½ bets. From the big blind it would be worth a call, but not from the small blind. The danger of domination is too great. K♦-Q♦ would be okay to call.

4a) Raise. A pair of tens is a decent hand against limpers, and you would like to keep the number of opponents down to maximise the chance of winning without improving.

4b) Raise. These suited high card combinations are much stronger when no-one has raised ahead of you, as the danger of domination by A-K or A-Q is very much less.

4c) Call. With two players already in you are not worried about a raise behind you, as this pot looks like being contested at least four-handed and it could easily be five or six. You have excellent implied odds to hit your set. However, you want to have callers here so you do not want to scare players off with a raise.

4d) Fold. This hand is just too weak. If you could be certain that no-one would raise then a call is just about okay. However, there are a lot of players still to speak, and you do not want to pay two bets to speculate with such a weak hand. The pair of threes you have in '4c' is a much more robust hand and can stand a call quite easily.

Odds Tables

It is useful to be aware of a few probabilities when playing hold'em. We have already looked at various scenarios earlier in the book and the material here will consolidate this knowledge

Starting Hands

There is no particular reason why you need to know starting hand probabilities in order to play successfully. However, these figures are interesting as it shows how rare decent starting hands really are. There will be times playing hold'em when you find you are just sitting there folding hand after hand after hand. These figures give some idea as to why this can happen.

The odds of being dealt:

Pocket aces **220-to-1 (0.45%)**

Any pocket pair **16-to-1 (5.9%)**

A-K suited **331-to-1 (0.3%)**

A-K offsuit **110-to-1 (0.9%)**

A-K suited or offsuit **82-to-1 (1.2%)**

Any two suited cards **3.3-to-1 (24%)**

Either pocket aces or pocket kings **110-to-1 (0.9%)**

Either pocket aces, pocket kings or A-K **46-to-1 (2.1%)**

Either pocket aces, pocket kings, pocket queens, A-K, A-Q or K-Q **19-to-1 (5%)**

Any pocket pair or two cards ten or higher **4.5-to-1 (18%)**

If you take a pocket pair to the river, you have a **4.2-to-1 (19%)** chance of making a set or better.

If you take two suited cards to the river, you have a **15-to-1 (6.4%)** chance of making a flush in your suit by then.

The Flop

These figures are useful in that they give you an idea about how likely your hand is to improve on the flop. As you can see, not many hands actually improve that much, which merely serves to emphasize how important it is to play only decent hands in the first place. Again, when you find that you are receiving an endless succession of miserable flops, you are not necessarily being terribly unlucky – it is just quite hard to get a good flop.

The odds of improving to:

A set or better from a pocket pair **7.5-to-1 (11.8%)**

A flush from two suited cards **118-to-1 (0.84%)**

A four-flush from two suited cards **8.1-to-1 (10.9%)**

A straight from two connecting cards **76-to-1 (1.3%)**

An eight out (open-ended or belly buster) straight draw from two connecting cards **9.4-to-1 (9.6%)**

A gutshot straight draw from two connecting cards **5.1-to-1 (16.6%)**

At least a pair (using pocket cards) from two non-pair cards **2.1-to-1 (32.4%)**

Two pair (using both pocket cards) from two non-pair cards **49-to-1 (2%)**

Post-Flop Improvement

The following figures are all useful in terms of calculating outs and consequently pot odds. The section 'from flop to river' obviously considers the chance of an improvement over two betting rounds rather than one. However, a knowledge of these figures is useful if you are thinking of playing a drawing hand hard, or maybe raising for a free card.

From Flop to Turn. Odds of improving to:

A full house or better from a set on the next card (7 outs) **5.7-to-1 (15%)**

A full house from two pair on the next card (4 outs) **11-to-1 (9%)**

A set from one pair on the next card (2 outs) **23-to-1 (4.3%)**

A flush from a four-flush on the next card (9 outs) **4.2-to-1 (19%)**

A straight from an open-ended draw on the next card (8 outs) **4.9-to-1 (17%)**

A straight from a gutshot draw on the next card (4 outs) **11-to-1 (9%)**

A pair from two non-pair cards (overcards) on the next card (6 outs) **6.8-to-1 (13%)**

From Flop to River. Odds of improving to:

A full house or better from a set by the river **2-to-1 (33%)**

A full house or better from two pair by the river (4 outs) **5.1-to-1 (17%)**

A set or better from one pair by the river (2 outs) **11-to-1 (8.4%)**

A flush from a four-flush by the river (9 outs) **1.9-to-1 (35%)**

A straight from an open-ended draw by the river

(8 outs) **2.2-to-1 (32%)**

A straight from a gutshot straight draw by the river
(4 outs) **5.1-to-1 (17%)**

A pair or better from two non-pair cards by the river
(6 outs) **3.2-to-1 (24%)**

From Turn to River. Odds of improving to:

A full house or better from a set on the final card
(10 outs) **3.6-to-1 (22%)**

A full house from two pair on the final card (4 outs)
11-to-1 (9%)

A set from one pair on the final card (2 outs) **22-to-1
(4.4%)**

A flush from a four-flush on the final card (9 outs)
4.1-to-1 (20%)

A straight from an open-ended draw on the final card
(8 outs) **4.8-to-1 (17%)**

A straight from a gutshot draw on the final card
(4 outs) **11-to-1 (9%)**

Glossary

Aggressive
A style of play that involves betting and raising rather than checking and calling (see page 182).

All-in
A player who is in a pot but has no more money to bet, or to call bets, is 'all-in'.

Backdoor
To make a hand (usually a flush or straight) by using both the turn and river cards.

Bad beat
A pot that is lost very much against the odds.

Bankroll
The money you have available to play poker.

Blank
A card which arrives on the turn or river and is of no help to anyone (see page 200).

Board
The cards showing on the table (see page 12).

Button
The dealer and the player to speak last on all post-flop rounds.

Call cold
To call two or more bets without having already invested money on a particular betting round.

Call down
To play a heads-up situation by simply calling all bets by the opponent with the aim of reaching a showdown.

Cap
To make the third raise on a betting round after which no further raising – on that round – is possible (see page 71).

Check-raise
To check and then raise when the opponent bets (see page 196).

Connectors
Cards of adjacent rank, e.g. 6-5, K-Q.

Counterfeit
When a card appears that kills all or part of your holding. For example, the board is A-J-9-3 and you hold A-3 and have two pair. If the river is a jack your second pair is counterfeit and is thus worthless.

Crying call
To call on the river without any great hope of your hand being good, usually when you have just been outdrawn.

Cut-off
The position before the button.

Dominated (hand)
A dominated hand is one where an 'improving' card doesn't help as it also makes the opponent's hand stronger. For example, A-K dominates K-J as hitting a king does not help the latter hand.

Double belly-buster
A double gutshot draw, for example J-10 with a board of A-Q-8 when either a king or nine will complete a straight.

Draw, drawing hand
A hand that has a reasonable chance to improve, usually to a straight or a flush.

Early position
The first three players to speak, pre-flop, in a full ring game of ten players.

Fish
A weak player, usually playing in a loose/passive style.

Fold
To throw away one's hand.

Free card
To receive a card without having had to invest money in the pot (see page 193).

Freeroll
To be splitting the pot but with a chance to improve to a winning hand. For example, if you have K♠-Q♠ and your opponent has K♥-Q♣ with a board of A♠-J♦-10♠. You both hold the top straight and it is impossible for you to lose the pot. However, you have a chance (with any spade) to improve to a flush and thus win.

Full ring game
A game with all ten players at the table.

Get away (from a hand)
To fold a decent, but worse, hand and avoid losing extra bets.

Getting (giving) heat
When pressure is applied with bets and raises.

Gutshot
A draw to a straight relying on just one card, e.g. 6-5 with a board of 8-9-K is hoping for a seven to complete the straight (see also *open-ended*).

Hand history
The details of the hand that has just been played. This only applies to online play. A key feature of this is that (on most sites) it is possible to see what a player was holding if they lost a showdown on the river. In live play a losing player rarely has to reveal their hand in this way.

Handle
The name (usually pseudonym) used by an online player.

Heads-up
A pot contested between two players.

Implied odds
The odds you can expect from a pot due to potential future action (see page 131).

Junk
A worthless hand.

Kicker
The sidecard to the main hand. For example, you hold A-K and an opponent A-J. The board is A-9-8-4-2. You both have a pair of aces but you win with your sidecard: your king kicker beating his jack kicker (see page 21).

Late blind
A player who joins a game has the option of posting a 'late blind' (in any non-blind seat other than the button) rather than waiting for the big blind to come round to them. This is usually done from the cut-off seat.

Late position
The cut-off and button seats.

Lead out
To be first to speak and bet on any post-flop betting round.

Leak
A negative feature of one's play that – in the long run – loses money (see page 149).

Limp
To call the big blind pre-flop rather than raising.

Loose
To play too many hands.

Maniac
A player who bets and raises much more than is justified by their holdings.

Middle position
The seats between early position and late position, typically the 4th, 5th and 6th seats after the blinds in a ten-player ring game.

Muck
To throw away your hand.

Nut(s)
A currently unbeatable hand. Also used are nut straight and nut flush for the best hand in those categories (see page 59).

Offsuit
Cards of differing suits.

On tilt
To play recklessly, usually after suffering unfortunate losses (see page 248).

Open-ended
A draw to a straight where there are two possible cards to complete the draw, e.g. 10-9 with a board of J-8-2. Here either a queen or a seven will complete the straight (see also *gutshot*).

Outdraw
To receive a card which improves your hand, so that you now are beating your opponent.

-outer (e.g. four-outer)
A hand which has a precise number of outs, e.g. a gutshot draw – requiring a card of a certain rank – is a four-outer.

Outkick
To beat an opponent who holds the same hand as you thanks to a better sidecard (see also *kicker*).

Outs
Cards which will improve your hand – possibly turning it into a winner (see pages 91, 109).

Overcard(s)
Card(s) ranking higher than any of the board cards.

Overpair
A pair ranking higher than any of the board cards.

Passive
A style of play relying on checking and calling rather than betting and raising (see page 12).

Pay-off hand
A hand which is too good to fold but is nevertheless second best, and thus results in you 'paying off' your opponent.

(to) Play back
To suddenly become the aggressor having previously been passive in the pot.

Position
Your seat at the table relative to your opponent(s) (see page 133).

Pot Equity
What the pot is currently 'worth' to you, based on the quality of your hand relative to those of your opponent(s) (see page 151).

Pot odds
The size of the pot relative to the size of the bet you are facing. Pot odds are used to calculate whether calling a bet represents good value (see page 126).

Protect(ing) a hand
Betting or raising with a good, but vulnerable holding (see page 193).

Quads
Four of a kind.

Rags
Low cards that most likely do not connect with players' hands.

Rainbow
A flop which features three different suits (so that a flush draw is not possible) is a rainbow flop.

Rake
The percentage of the pot taken by the house (or online site). Online this is typically $1-$3 per pot (see page 84).

Read
To figure out (correctly or otherwise) what cards the opponents hold.

Redraw
The turn card improves an opponent's holding such that they now have the best hand. You then improve on the river to beat them.

Reload
To bring more money to the table after you have lost your stack.

Represent
To suggest a certain holding by your betting and/or raising.

Re-raise
To raise in response to a raise.

Rock
A very tight player.

Rockets
Aces.

Runner-runner
To make a hand by receiving helpful cards on both the turn and the river.

Semi-bluff
To bluff when you also have some chance to improve to the best hand (see page 219).

Set
Three of a kind made by having a pair in your hand which matches a board card (see page 46).

Short-handed
A game featuring few players, typically five or less.

Short-stacked
To run short of money on the table, so that you may find yourself 'all-in' at some point during a pot.

Showdown
When the cards are revealed at the end of the hand.

Side pot
A side pot is created when one player is 'all-in' and has no further funds to bet or call bets. The all-in player competes only for the main pot, and the other players in the hand compete for both the main pot and the side pot.

Slowplay
To bet timidly – checking and/or calling – to represent weakness when actually holding a strong hand (see page 222).

Stack
The money you have available on the table.

Steal
To win the pot without any hand at all simply by betting and everyone else folding.

Steaming
To play over-aggressively, usually after losing a big pot.

Strong
A style of play which is typically tight/aggressive (see page 14).

Tainted outs
Cards that improve your hand, but unfortunately give an opponent an even stronger hand (see page 97).

Texture
The degree to which the board is coordinated, allowing straight and flush possibilities (see page 56).

Tight
A style of play whereby a player plays very few hands (see page 11).

Trap hand
A hand which, by its nature, causes you to lose money.

Trash
A worthless hand.

Trips
Three of a kind made by having a card in your hand which matches a pair on the board (see page 27).

Under-the-gun (UTG)
The player first to speak in the pre-flop betting round.

Weak
A style of play which is typically loose/passive (see page 14).

Whiplash
To be whiplashed is to call a bet or raise and then face a further raise (or raises) on the same betting round.